HUDDLING

HUDDLING

The Informal Way to Management Success

V. Dallas Merrell

A DIVISION OF AMERICAN MANAGEMENT ASSOCIATIONS

Library of Congress Cataloging in Publication Data

Merrell, V   Dallas, 1936–
  Huddling: the informal way to management success.

  Bibliography: p.
  Includes index.
  1. Management. 2. Interpersonal relations.
3. Organizational behavior. I. Title.
HD38.M427   658.4   78-31941
ISBN 0-8144-5506-9

First Printing

*Organizations work when people huddle
to get results*

TO
Spencer W. Kimball,
his predecessors and successors,
with whom I have dedicated
my life and loyalty

Preface

THIS book has been an unusual personal and professional experience: an outflowing of ideas that were unplanned and unusually spontaneous. It represents what I have been encountering in the "real world" for years. But the concepts I had acquired and developed over the years were inadequate to describe and explain these experiences, although I had worked through three graduate degrees in the behavioral and management sciences, read much of the literature, had a stock of theories and conclusions, and used a repertoire of strategies and techniques to serve my clients. I had found that much of what was "on the market" did not fit the *realities* and the *needs* of organizational workers, thousands of whom have asked me privately and publicly: "How can I do better? What can I do to make a difference, to get results?"

Huddling came to me as a burst of insight, a stream of ideas, not through a chain of logic. With huddling as a central notion many other things fell into place. It started in 1975 as I stepped temporarily out of my normal work activities and into a presidential political maelstrom. I still have the initial one-page outline of the huddling ideas that I scribbled down while standing amid the turbulent crowd during the national nominating convention. The book came later during an abortive attempt to rest in the West. That trip ended with three or four days of around-the-clock dictation and a manuscript in hand. A year later, in 1978, I returned to the West and tinkered with the text until I was ready to turn it loose to critics and a publisher.

Enough for sentimental and professional backtracking. However, my comments about how this happened are not completely irrelevant to the subject. Huddling is experiential and takes place within the context of disorderly conducted commerce, and it is both personal and consequential.

This is a professional biography of sorts, a report of my own insights, conclusions, and experience. It describes what I see happening in organizations and what I think can be done about it. The huddling techniques described are based on my experience as a leader in huddle-laden organizations. They draw heavily on my work as executive coach for thousands of huddlers and nonhuddlers. I have also benefited from bits and pieces of literature, studies, and theories relevant to this subject.

In writing about huddling, I've had in mind all those organizational workers whose work involves direct contact with other people: some laborers, technical workers, supervisors, executives, politicians, management specialists, and professionals. The ideas seem to help even those at home who regularly send workers off to the job and absorb some of their frustrations at the end of the working day. New as well as established workers can benefit. I've been told that every responsible participant in our organizational society needs to understand huddling processes. I agree.

I would be most pleased to learn how these ideas fit with your own experiences, and to receive your ideas for improving the descriptions and prescriptions I have presented here.

Best wishes for your success.

V. Dallas Merrell

Acknowledgments

Many thanks to Karen Dixon, an at-home huddler whose husband I am proud to be; to Ann, Kay, Joan, Paul Dixon, Mary, Mark Jensen, John Carter, Ilene, and David Porter—our children with whom we run our family enterprise, literally, as a nationwide huddling network; to Kent S. Larsen, for his encouragement and valuable criticism; to Bertram C. Willis, William C. Rock, R. Wayne Shute, and Jean C. Dixon, who read and helped to revise an early draft; to Mary Merrell, Nicky Horne, and Myrleen Post, who typed thoughtfully and built my confidence in the product; to Samuel B. Marks, Robert J. Zenowich, and Eric Valentine of AMA, who facilitated the finished product; and to William G. Dyer, Frank P. Sherwood, and Chester A. Newland, colleagues who tutored me in earlier years and whose influence continues today.

I am especially grateful to the many industrial and public executives who have asked me for personal counsel and practical ideas. In their persistent search for ways to improve their performance as leaders, they have prodded me to translate philosophies into principles and principles into practices, to convert theories into the take-home strategies and skills that can benefit the vital institutions they seek to serve. I thank them and pay tribute to all those who are trying to be better leaders and performers in worthwhile pursuits.

Contents

I
Huddling Insights

*H*UDDLING is an important but little known phenomenon pervasive in society. Huddlers are the responsible workers who get results. By understanding
huddling you can better understand how you stack up,
how to improve your productivity, and how to help
your co-workers get more done and gain more satisfaction from jobs well done.

1
Huddling

ORGANIZATIONS don't work well normally.
Everyone knows that. Throughout our lives virtually
all of us confront perplexing, formalistic, phlegmatic
organizations—hospitals, schools, governments, businesses, banks, postal services, unions, and so on. Yet
some organizational workers manage to accomplish
much more than others, to get results in spite of the
formal organization. Sometimes we forget that organizations don't get results; people do! *People in huddles
usually accomplish the most significant work in organizations.*

Huddling Observed

Let's look briefly at how huddlers manage to get
things done in organizations:

3

□ A business executive is about to go into an important meeting with other company executives. He huddles for a few moments with a trusted assistant to make sure that everything is in order and that they are both up to date on what they are going to do. After the meeting two vice-presidents walk through the hall to their offices, huddling informally to confirm the fact that a given proposal made in the meeting is contrary to their best interests.

□ A student sticks his head in a professor's door and in less than 30 seconds gets the professor to agree on what will happen in the next class. The student does this by making a suggestion and offering to do a task that will make it easy for the professor to implement the suggestion.

□ Government leaders are entertained by business contracts at a hunting lodge or country club. The casual setting provides an excellent opportunity for influence to be exercised, decisions to be made, information to be shared, and plans to be jelled.

□ A presidential candidate meets many people across the country in face-to-face encounters, discussing issues, sharing campaign plans, and soliciting their involvement. Subsequent exposure through television and other media solidify the campaign, but the extensive huddling beforehand paved the way for the campaign's success.

□ New farming practices are introduced into a community through "opinion leaders," those whose judgments are respected by other farmers. Discussions about new techniques take place through the informal interactions among farmers, and between farmers and suppliers. It is through these huddles that farmers share information and experiences, and obtain assurances from influential people that a new practice or a new piece of machinery is in their best interests.

A Burst of Insight

I discovered huddling after I was invited to assume a management role for a presidential candidate during the 1975 national nominating convention. As it turned out, this was an extremely intense activity working with a short-lived organization. Conflict and stress were acute. The behind-the-scenes work was to have an important effect on winning or losing the nomination for the presidency. Normal management controls were lacking. Virtually everyone was a volunteer, and authoritarian tactics would not work. Although a formal organization had been outlined, published, and taped to a wall, the *real* management was not described in the organization chart.

As the various political activities unfolded, I found myself struggling to understand the experience and compare it with normal business and bureaucratic processes. At first my reaction was, "How different!" But gradually I began to see unmistakable connections between that volatile, turbulent situation and more typical organizational and management activities. Eventually I could find no significant differences between the management of this presidential organization and other organizations with which I normally work. The program at the convention was literally run in huddles—a powerful concept that describes how things work everywhere else in organizations.

I've observed and worked with huddles in government departments and agencies, industrial and business establishments, associations and research groups. I've seen the same concepts apply in civic and voluntary organizations and in social institutions such as schools, health establishments, families, professional offices, and political organizations. *Virtually every organization I know is run in huddles.* I do not advocate huddles as such. I don't need to. They go on all around us, everywhere. Huddles are natural events. They are intelligent acts by responsible participants trying to get results. This is not to suggest that organizations do not need structure, legal authority, management controls, and information systems. Leaders and the rank and file must work with *both* the formal and informal organization to make things run as well as possible. But it is the informal features of organizational work—the operations that are least understood and most frustrating to many workers—that are the source of fruitful results for others.

Huddling Defined

A *huddle is a temporary, intimate, work-oriented encounter between two or more people.* Huddlers draw together informally and confer, "nestling" to get results where organizations fail. A huddle is the source of considerable information, the locus of significant decisions, the setting for power transactions, the place where many responsibilities get defined, and the impetus for motivating people to get things done. Huddles compensate for countless organizational ineptitudes.

Huddles are not so much the grease for oiling the organizational machine as they are the buzz saw that allows intelligent individuals to cut through organizational debris and clutter. Responsible huddling demands an attitude expressed by Samuel Johnson: "To do something is in everyone's power."

Huddles satisfy a critical need for the organization to get results rather than to deal interminably in processes. A simple social encounter is not a huddle: it is not goal-oriented, purposeful. Huddles are a critical aspect of any organization. They are to the informal organization what business meetings are to the official, formal organization.

It may be going too far to say a huddle is a social system that is enduring or set. A huddle is more like a fragile social web—episodic (coming and going intermittently) and epitasic (where the action is developed in a drama)—an epitask (a fragmented but consequential part of a job).

The member of the board of directors of a large business organization recently underscored the validity of huddling theory. Their board meetings, he reported, ratify decisions already made informally behind the scenes by the officers involved. All the directors know how they are going to vote on the propositions. The outcome of a meeting is determined in various huddles before it is ever held.

A huddle by nature is simple and unobtrusive. It involves few people. Normally, it is a fleeting event, lasting a few seconds or at most a few minutes. Huddles are based on trust—with minimal complicity or suspicion.

Communication in a huddle is highly efficient. Words and symbols are clear to those participating, including a tailor-made shorthand vocabulary. In the huddle, partners can say, "Let's do it. I'll back you all the way." To attempt to do the same in the official organization may require carefully drawn protective legal documents and prolonged exchanges of memoranda and ideas.

Trappings of the office are not needed. A minimum of verbal interaction is usually sufficient. Indeed, a huddle may be one of the most focused and efficient of organizational phenomena. Usually only a few matters are covered in a given huddle, and each is specific as to the results sought—whether it be information sharing, coordination, decision making, or planning.

In practice, some huddles are *continuing*— individuals repeatedly and regularly meet to deal with matters of common concern. Others are *intermittent*—occasionally involving the same people but occurring irregularly. Still others are *isolated*. People huddle to handle a given matter and then disperse, never meeting again on the issue.

Sometimes huddles are closely aligned to the official organization, as when vice-presidents huddle with each other and their president. At other times the organization is so out of tune with reality—so divorced from the needs and habits of workers—that huddles make significant departures from formal organizational patterns. Here the president is unable to trust and communicate with a vice-president and, instead, bypasses him and deals directly but unofficially with remote subordinates. President John F. Kennedy often startled unsuspecting bureaucrats by calling them directly; he felt information might get distorted if it was carried through normal channels. In either case, it can be argued that huddling is operationally a rational process, achieving ends by the *best available* means.

Inclusion

Who are huddle members? Rather than speaking of membership in a huddle, it is more accurate to think in terms of *inclusion*. People do not join or apply for a huddle; they are included. They do not petition for membership; they are consulted or involved. Inclusion can be a highly subtle matter, particularly since most people have no conscious awareness that huddles exist. Nevertheless, those who exercise influence in organizations work effectively in huddles and know when they are involved or cut off from participation.

Authority and Control

Authority in a huddle comes from assertiveness. *Assertive authority* is that influence derived from the dynamic, productive actions of a huddler. This authority is not necessarily related to any legal rights or formal position. A person who has very little formally delegated authority may "exercise" immense influence and credibility because of the ability to get things done, to move in and do a tough job. Often, what nonhuddlers lack is commitment, a streak of gall and stamina.

A huddler operates and exercises influence within a *working enclave*. This territory or working space may be larger or smaller than the huddler's official position.

Control in huddles is positive rather than negative. *Affirmative control* comes from arousing people's interest, nurturing their commitments, and involving them in projects and activities that make them feel productive and give them psychological rewards. It requires building on people's natural drives and inclinations and then channeling their contributions toward productive ends.

Contemporary management theorists often suggest that the official organization operate more like the in-

formal organization, imitating its strong points—for
example, seating people in meetings so they can see
each other to facilitate participation and exchange;
taking workers' feelings into consideration and using
their natural talents to build motivation; improving
supervisory skills in assertiveness, communications,
and human relations; using group problem-solving
techniques; and applying simulation processes to pre-
test the leadership abilities of candidates for promotion into management. Through these and other ways,
the notion of assertive leadership is applied by organizations.

Demise

Huddling is vulnerable to changes in relationships
and personnel. Huddles have no "legal right" of exis-
tence through formal organizational charters or position descriptions. Therefore, they may change with
whim or fancy or with the loss of key participants
through retirement, termination, transfer, or lack of
interest.

Huddling opportunities are forever perishable. Relationships, alliances, working partnerships must continually be forged. Deterioration must be detected
and deterred. Misunderstandings must be rectified.
Participants must be given some kind of psychological
payoff, if not other rewards. Huddling depends so
much on other people that personalities need to be
reckoned with if productive, intensive interactions are
to continue.

Huddling Institutions

Upper-class institutions service the huddling
needs of society's elite. The Cosmos Club of

Washington, D.C., takes pride in its members and its influence on public policy. The expense and exclusiveness of membership in the Century Association of New York City are defended because of the contacts and contracts forged there. The Duquesne Club of Pittsburgh, Union League of Philadelphia, Capital City Club of Atlanta, and Metropolitan Club of Washington, D.C., share similar functions for huddling among America's elite.

Other institutions for huddling include country clubs, golf courses, professional associations, conventions, business offices, and fraternal organizations. Huddling goes on in neighborhood bars, car pools, and pool halls, over coffee counters and lunch bucket breaks. Huddlers conspire in union halls and on street corners.

Each huddle functions according to its needs, bringing together those who have common commerce and concerns and providing the exclusivity, atmosphere, and services needed to achieve its goals. In effect, huddlers make the organization work by using the strengths of various people outside the formal organizational structure. Huddling may well be the ultimate form of "organizational democracy." Participation is based on competence and contribution, on natural checks and balances. The processes are responsible, open, and continually evolving to meet real needs.

Huddling is a fortuitous fusion of two ethics: a work ethic that espouses energetic efforts to achieve results and a social ethic that suggests that workers ought to get along with others, to succeed in interpersonal relationships. The conjugal outcome can be called the "results ethic" of huddling.

Now, as you read this book, keep in mind that *organizations work when people huddle to get results!*

2
Huddling Roots

THE roots of huddling are familiar to all of us. Every organization is perpetually reorganizing itself, unaware that all organizations—not just the present organization—do not work well. *An organization is more akin to a contraption than to a smooth-running machine.*

Most sizable organizations—business and industrial organizations as well as government agencies—are in reality tangled bureaucracies. Organizational ecology has become so complex that "informal" practices and working relationships emerge to make things simpler, to make them work. Organizations are permeated with private caucuses devoted to breaking deadlocks and getting things done.

Formal Versus Informal Features

The formal organization consists of legal charters, bylaws, manuals, job descriptions, formal delegations of authority, budgets, brochures, organization charts, files, written plans, reports, correspondence, meetings, facilities, technologies, products and services, contracts, logotypes, and other legal–official artifacts—designed, engineered entities.

By contrast, the informal organization is a mixture of personalities, understandings, expectations, customs, taboos, alliances, deferences, feelings, and activities—organizational "culture." These evolve naturally out of the needs of workers and out of the relationships and activities that occur within the framework of the formal organization.

The formal features of the organization are often quite conspicuous and are presumed by many people to dictate the way things actually work. Informal features are far less obvious but play a significant role in how work gets done. In this regard, we can look at a case study used by the Harvard Graduate School of Business. The case presents a typical example of how the official organization is supplemented by the unofficial.

The Dashman Company, a large military equipment manufacturer, had over 20 plants dispersed through the central United States. Procurement of supplies and materials had never been centrally coordinated. Facing the possibility of a shortage of raw materials, a vice-president for purchasing issued a written directive ordering the centralization of purchases over $10,000. The purchasing vice-president was new to his job and had met only a few of the plant executives. The president and board or directors formally approved the plan.

The directive seemed to be received favorably, judging by written plant manager replies that they would be cooperative. However, over the next six weeks (the biggest buying period of the year) none of the plant managers notified the central office about pending contracts as required by the new policy. Central office executives who traveled to the plants reported that each plant was busy, that there were no shortages of raw materials, and that the usual routines for that season were being followed. It seems clear that the plant executives had informal alternatives worked out among themselves—undoubtedly through huddling by phone or in person—about how purchasing would be handled.

The formal features of organizations frequently fail to fit the needs of workers and the realities of working life. This chapter examines some of these features and why they give rise to huddling activities.

Job Layers

Most workers are buried under layers of positions. Formal authority increases as you go up the hierarchy. In order for something to get done in the official system, orders or authorizations come from the top down, with reporting normally being passed back up through several levels of the organization. The people at these various levels have divergent opinions, personalities, interests, and functions to perform.

In many ways—known to most who will read this book—the officialdom of organizations often gets in the way of doing the very thing that it is charged to do.

Because of the many layers of authority, organizations usually are slow to respond. Messages are revised and changed as they are passed up or down the different organizational layers, and are restricted by official rules and procedures.

In the late 1960s George Romney, then Secretary of Housing and Urban Development, visited the Fouteenth Street corridor in Washington, D.C., after the burning and rioting. Romney made a dramatic pronouncement on the spot that the government would respond immediately to rebuild and restore the neighborhood. The years of inaction and ineffectiveness that followed attest to the obstacles created by the layers of authority, rules, and regulations of the official organization.

Obsolescence

Virtually every organization is obsolete. For this reason, responsible workers often find it necessary to operate outside the prescribed channels of communication and decision making, to coalesce with others of like mind, and to find ways to get the job done in spite of the organization that was set up to do the job in the first place. These conditions lead to informal huddles, which become the medium for communication and coordination in the informal organization.

The situation is characterized by this report from one worker: "I was so mad. I couldn't get a decision so I could get my job done. I was tempted to let things go, so they could see what would happen. But when it came right down to it, I couldn't do that. I finally checked with Max, who was here before. He said he thought it would be safe to go ahead and get started without any fanfare. I went ahead and then casually

mentioned to my boss how things were going. He
never raised any red flags. Even though this isn't what
the manual says, things have worked out and we've
been doing it that way ever since."

Confusion

Most organizational participants struggle to establish a role and make some meaningful contribution.
They must work within a maze of shifting realities that
should dazzle the imagination of behavioral and management theorists. To the theorist this is "interesting."
To the person striving to be a responsible contributor,
it is a frustrating, demoralizing, perplexing experience. Shortly after taking office, John F. Kennedy reportedly commented that he was surprised to learn
things were as bad as he had been saying they were.

Most workers are unaware of how the significant
tasks of the organization get done. Few understand
either why things go wrong or how to make them better. Even more important, they don't understand why
things work when they do and are therefore unable to
replicate them to ensure that good working methods
are perpetuated.

Jimmy Carter campaigned for the presidency as a
Washington outsider and brought into government
many officials of like mind—aggressively suspicious of
the establishment. One man who had been very critical of federal programs came in to head an agency that
had complex nationwide programs and an $8 billion
budget. His previous management experience consisted in heading a public-interest group with a staff of
three. When he took over he brought with him two
trusted staff associates. This was part of the problem.
Not only did he lack essential management skills; he

failed to open huddling relations with powerful, established program leaders.

The bureaucratic power structure generally was hospitable to the new man and ready to work with him. But the frustration of being shut off was aggravated by the fact that the administrator had an intense, exclusive huddling relationship with his two bright, but inexperienced assistants. None of the three developed huddling linkages with those workers in the organization who could help them most. They remained outsiders at a time when they could have won considerable internal support for their programs.

Personalities

Huddles also emerge because of personality differences among those who occupy positions of authority in the formal organization. Most people are reluctant to share vital information with others whom they do not trust. Trust does not automatically result when two people are placed in formal positions that call for interaction. Even if the two people do trust each other, they may find it difficult to work together if they have incompatible, "odd couple" working styles. For instance, one person may be systematic in approaching a job; the other may be more impetuous and intuitive. Often, even though these people judge each other to be honest and honorable, they derive no satisfaction from their formally prescribed working relationships.

This is not to suggest that "sameness" is necessary or desirable in working relationships. What is needed is compatibility—people with complementary skills and working styles who can combine their diverse talents to get things done.

A secretary described her new boss's takeover as

division director at NASA headquarters. In inheriting
the official organization, he discovered some urgent
tasks left undone. He quickly assessed the competent,
reliable talent in the organization. He then handed out
the tough assignments to those few he felt he could
trust, regardless of their formal positions. Some ill
feeling was evident, but the informal group rose to the
challenge and got the big tasks done as scheduled.

Diverse Society

Many points of view, interests, and approaches are
proposed for carrying out social functions. This diversity in our society is repeated in each complex
organization. But in order for organizations to function, people must get together with others who are
involved in common activities, combining their efforts
and reducing the tensions between them. Because of
the informality provided in huddling, it is easier for
these needed adjustments to be made.

Huddling facilitates highly pragmatic adaptations
in our diverse society so that problems can be resolved and institutions can be more productive.

Born Followers

Many people are promoted inappropriately into
leadership positions. I estimate that 98 percent of organizational workers lack essential leadership skills.
I've worked with organizations where over two-thirds
of those nominated for management assignments were
unfit for leadership responsibilities. Normally, candidates for office—whether public servants or organizational leaders—are evaluated on the basis of their past
record. But past performance is not a certain indica-

tion of how people will perform in the future, particularly when new positions call for leadership ability on the job.

Most promotions in organizations are made on the basis of technical proficiency, which is generally easier to evaluate than leadership potential. Therefore, many people who end up in responsible positions are unable to provide the leadership demanded. Huddling arises to fill in the leadership gaps in organizations and to ensure that the work gets done.

Risk Reduction

Most organizational workers prefer to reduce the risks involved in their actions. Few intelligent people perch out on a limb needlessly. It is safer to first work things out behind the scenes unofficially before "going public." Through huddling, a few concerned individuals can caucus to reach a decision, make arrangements, and test their proposal to make sure it will work before they make it official.

In huddles, people can make certain they "have the guns" before they go to war. Prudence requires checking risks, attitudes, experiences, resources, timing, and handicaps. *Huddling is a strategy for reducing surprise.*

Not long ago a merger of two giant corporations thrust a new entity into the *Fortune* 500. An insider reported that the deal was forged while the principals were "casting flies at the E. R. Harriman Ranch in Idaho." This environment allowed the participants to explore ideas out of the view of others and to reduce the risks that were involved at this stage of the negotiations.

Power Diffuseness

Real power is almost always shared by many people. Power is diffuse. In every organization or social situation any one person—even a top legal authority—has only limited power to dictate *how* things are done or even *what* should be done. Likewise, no one person has the power to stop things from happening. All organizational workers suffer because of the gap between what they want to happen and what they can get to happen. This gap occurs in spite of job descriptions and formal delegations of authority.

Because of the diffuseness of power, almost anyone can have some measure of influence over the work of the organization. Influence in any organization, at any level, is up for grabs. Out of this grow the informal working relationships, the networks of power and control, the array of huddlers and huddling relationships. Huddling is the process by which participants work at winning and exercising their share of power.

Management Systems

Organizations cannot really be managed or controlled; they can only be shepherded and entreated toward a multiplicity of competing personal and organizational goals. Formal management systems are rarely understood by workers and often do not conform even closely to the ways things really happen.

Whenever careful attention is paid to organizing and delegating in an organization, responsibility and initiative seem to sink out of sight. Management systems don't get work done; huddlers do. Responsible huddlers work with and through other people as best they can. Huddling is the process by which "the people" work to get results.

President Lyndon Johnson had more faith in huddling than in formal meetings. He would call a Cabinet meeting to order and set things in motion, then wheel about, get on the phone, and carry on the "real" business of the presidency.

3
Huddle Watching

*H*ow do you recognize a huddle when you see one? What do you look and listen for? Huddles have a number of distinctive characteristics.

Obscurity

Huddles are obscure, but found virtually everywhere. You can note significant decisions being made at the water cooler, on the golf course, after hours in somebody's office. During a meeting break you may see two or three individuals casually congregate. They may well be agreeing on a critical decision for the organization.

A manager leaves a meeting and is met in the hall by one of her assistants or by a colleague from elsewhere in the organization; they spend a working moment huddling as they walk through the hall to her office. Many huddles occur on the phone as two individuals touch base to make sure they are in agreement. People huddle in car pools, sharing information that is used during working hours. Huddling occurs as one individual passes another a formal report with an accompanying comment or gesture that carries important meanings.

Most huddles take place unobtrusively before or after other, more visible events. Significant events often happen between scheduled and more high-profile meetings, and sometimes during a break or a lull in a formal meeting. Huddling occurs as one person slips in for a moment before another person is to start the next meeting. Because of the efficient nature of a huddle, significant tasks can be accomplished in only a brief moment. One businessman tells how two executives reached a multi-million-dollar decision while taking a break in the men's room between meetings.

Proximity

People huddle when they are in close proximity. Different cultures define "close" differently. Generally, however, a huddle takes place within the sphere of people's personal space, but not so close as to intrude into their private space. If people are standing far apart it is unlikely that they are in a real huddle— unless it is occurring on the phone or through a "thumbs up" signal at a distance (probably a confirmation of some previous huddle). This physical closeness allows for lowered voices, more private communications, and a sense of togetherness that would be lacking at distances.

Consider, too, how people are seated or arranged.

Huddles do not normally take place in an orderly seating or standing pattern. While those involved are likely to be close, you will probably observe a somewhat random distribution among primary participants in the huddle.

Small Numbers

The larger the number of people, the less likely they are to be in a huddle. In large groups relationships tend to become more formal and trust decreases. Huddles are probably going on *within* a large group, but not by the group as a whole.

Arrangement on Demand

Most huddles are unscheduled. A meeting that has been set up for some time is not likely to be a true huddle. Huddles are "organic," arising to meet existing demands. Such demands usually are not predictable enough to allow for scheduling.

But we cannot dismiss scheduled huddles altogether. Some managers set regular times for meetings without precisely identifying what is to be covered. Therefore, if a scheduled huddle exists, we can predict that the longer the lead time for scheduling, the less precise the matters discussed.

A huddle is arranged more by the question "Got a minute?" or "Which way you walking?" than by "Do you think I could set up a meeting with you?" or "See my secretary and see if we can work it in."

Brevity

Huddles vary greatly in duration but are generally shorter than an official meeting. Many huddles are so fleeting that they pass unobserved or are mistaken for casual social encounters of little consequence. Some huddles are extended and cover a number of matters. Occasionally organizations will convene a *retreat*— extended huddles away from the more structured activities and environments of the formal organization. A professor colleague of mine, a consultant to a Cabinet officer in Washington, told of how he and a second-level official would sometimes slip out of a "heavy" meeting, take care of the very issue being discussed, and return with the decision made and set in motion before the meeting's end. Needless to say, they had consulted the powers that really mattered, then huddled effectively to produce the results that the official organization was going through the motions to handle.

Focus

Huddles are very focused events. That is, they are characterized by the rapt attentiveness of participants to the matter at hand. Although attention may shift, the togetherness of participants on the issue can be observed as a highly focused phenomenon.

A long-time associate of mine was elected president of a national professional organization. I was at the national conference briefly to present a paper when I learned of his election and spotted him in a crowd. We had not seen each other for some time, and I anticipated a spontaneous outburst of greeting as I approached. However, I had failed to notice that he was huddling with another colleague, evidently on a matter of importance. My old associate spotted me but ignored me momentarily. I stood by patiently until the intensely focused huddle was over. Then the enthusiastic reunion came as expected.

Lack of Documentation

Most huddles lack documentation of what occurs. In some cases, a preexisting paper, memorandum, or report may provide a stimulus for the huddle. In other cases, some scribbles may be produced as memory prodders for participants. But generally there are few documented "traces" of specific huddles. The Nixon tapes are an exception—and an illustration of the risks involved in documentation, particularly when devious or illegal activities are carried on in huddles. In this case, both the nature of the huddling and the documentation showed poor judgment.

Equality of Status

Most huddles will not display marked differences in status among those participating. A huddle is, in a very real sense, a leveling experience for those involved. Differences in status do exist, and some of those differences may be felt. Nevertheless, in most huddles few individuals are going to pull rank or make demands based on differences in authority or status. Participants are near equals—even if for the moment. If any differentiation exists, it is likely to be in roles rather than in status. Huddling provides an opportunity to reach down, across, up, and even outside the organization to involve people who can solve problems and make decisions—regardless of their status, rank, or position.

High-Risk Tasks

Huddles tend to take on the high-risk, core-sensitive, complex, essential tasks of the organization. The official organization is more inclined to be in-

volved in routine, low-risk adjustments and administrative matters. If no huddlers step forward to handle
the difficult tasks, the official organization will often
try to treat them as routine, administrative matters and
hide behind rules, procedures, and precedents. The
difference between these types of activities is significant and highlights the nature of the huddling process.

Informal Language

Communications become more simple as trust and
intimacy grow. Shorthand phrases, first names, and
nicknames are common in huddles. Language becomes simplified, and sentences tend to be ab-
breviated. Understanding comes quickly and increases as values and outlooks are shared by those
communicating with each other.

Much of the information required in a formal setting does not need to be covered in a huddle. Communications become more intricate as they are passed
formally up, down, and through the organization.
Communications in meetings, conferences, and lec-
tures are more laborious and complicated, and generally less effective, than those observed in huddling
situations.

Implicit Understanding

When huddlers are on the same wavelength and
have common understandings about problems, there
is no need for the excessive details and trappings of
formal communications.

In the movie *Turning Point,* the two ballet stars
practice together, stop a moment, and exchange looks
and feelings. Then the male lead says, "Let's go on."
And on they dance, picking it up precisely from where

they had halted. Masterful huddlers will understand
this point: the need for implicit understanding. Volumes of authoritative descriptions could not have
conveyed what the two dancers instantaneously understood. Verbal instructions would have required extensive knowledge of art, philosophy, and psychology,
along with anthropology and anatomy. As it was, they
took it from where they were, and both knew precisely
what to do.

When the judgment of others is respected, there is
less need to justify or explain that judgment, less need
to question the relevancy of facts or the validity of
evidence. Often huddle participants will have implicit trust in the soundness of a person's conclusions, recommendations, or suggestions. However,
background data, rationales, or arguments may be
needed so participants can adequately explain the
position to others.

Exchange

It should not be supposed that give-and-take is
missing in huddles. Vigorous discussion and examination of matters exist in all healthy working relationships. But in huddles these communications are less
complicated and more productive, and arise from significantly different circumstances than do communications in the formal organization. The language of a
huddle is typified by the following:

"We okay on this?"
"Shall we go on it?"
"Just tone it down a bit and I'll be with you."
"Tom was in here this morning. Here is how I
     think we've got to come across . . ."

"I think we've got a good package."

"I'll be here. Stop back after."

"I just don't feel good about that; here's an out if you want one."

It should also be apparent by people's language whether someone is being included in huddling activities. Some tipoffs that a person is getting the "cold shoulder" from the informal organization are:

"See John on that."

"You'll need to put it in writing and have it reviewed first."

"We'll have to take that up with the board in order to get a decision."

"Why bring that up now?"

"What does that have to do with me? Why bother me?"

"That's Joan's job. Why are you getting involved in it?"

"I can't help you."

4
Nonhuddlers

IN huddling, as elsewhere, counterfeits are often mistaken for the real thing. Some nonhuddlers are "backsliders" who have lost their way but can be brought back to the fold. Others can never be reclaimed.

To be an effective huddler, you must be cognizant of the various types of organizational inhabitants who do not work well in huddles. Awareness of these groups will help you avoid unproductive relations and activities. You should also recognize that huddlers face a double burden: they must handle the tasks before them as well as the nonhuddlers who stand in their way.

Hasslers

Hasslers are the ever ready hit men of the organization. They are skirmishers and sometimes tyrants who focus on fighting rather than results. They are excuse generators rather than problem solvers. Hassling may be prompted by some of the same motives as huddling, but it takes its direction from a reactive, negative attitude. Hasslers are self-protective, destructive game players and ruckus perpetuators. Conflict, disputation, putdowns, and estrangement are their products.

Hustlers

Hustlers are the scavengers of organizational life, feeding off others without giving anything of themselves. Hustling is the self-serving activity carried on aggressively by those looking out for No. 1. Hustlers are after every reward they can get—money, power, status, honor. They operate without regard for the needs of the organization and other people. Hustlers are the notorious office politicians, climbers, and robber barons of organizational society. While masking their motives and actions, they seek rewards without commensurate contributions to the productivity of the organization.

Butlers

Butlers are the organizational servants who take orders from others. They repeat what they are told to say, when and to whom. Their effectiveness depends on the skill and judgment of their masters. Their orders may come from a person—a boss, dominant peer, or controlling, superior subordinate—or from the "rules"—administrative procedures, regulations, precedents, and instructions to be followed unthinkingly. They run on borrowed power and play the stand-in role, though often they don't know how to convert the proxies they carry into profitable results.

Butlers are mechanical, reactive surrogates, rather than thinking people who can act intelligently on behalf of someone else. Too often they are called upon to be the carriers of bad news or hatchet men, doing another's dirty work. Butlers "sit in" rather than "being in." That is the root of their failure. Even though they may perform well, someone else is pulling the strings.

Cuddlers

For some, work life is a warm blanket. Cuddlers are dependent on others for their sense of security. They thrive on friendships, loving relations, sweet talk, cliques, and the niceties of social interaction. Graciously they gravitate to situations that involve other "people-oriented persons," but they do not seem to recognize the difference between a workplace and a country club. Often, they will put up with a modicum of work to gain the psychological reward of interpersonal relationships. Cuddlers avoid conflict and stress at any cost.

Muddlers

Without a clear vision of something to be achieved, muddlers are experts at moving away from undesirable situations. They are the epitome of adjustment, avoiding pain and conflict by making marginal accommodations. They are trouble avoiders rather than problem solvers or peacemakers. Muddlers expend energy not on getting results, but on staying out of hassles. Because of their hindward vision, they forever work in their own shadows. Success to them means making something less dismal than it might have been or skillfully avoiding a disastrous situation.

Mumblers

Mumblers have an idea of what needs to be done, but they lack the courage to make a firm commitment or the skills to contribute effectively. Mumblers mutter, hesitating with self-doubt. They set up verbal smokescreens to hide their indecision. They straddle the fence and play the middle of the street. Mumblers are chameleons who change color to fit the situation. They use communication to deflect or deceive, not to clarify. Co-workers never know quite where mumblers stand and come to disdain the ambiguity of their flex-values and transparent hues.

Scuttlers

Scuttlers tell you it can't be done, it's too hard, don't waste your time and effort, we've tried that before, it will set a bad precedent. They throw blocks before positive thinking and affirmative action. They will tell you that even though it's not really against the rules, it's not possible, it won't sell, the boss may not like it, it's too expensive, you may lose. Scuttlers specialize in delay tactics: it's the wrong time, you're not ready, let's think it over a while longer. Scuttlers always want another study. They pull the switch to throw an important matter on a sidetrack in the hope that it will be forgotten or ignored.

Coddlers

Some pseudo-charitable types expend their energies on protecting their fellow workers from the realities of organizational life. Coddlers have not learned that eventually people must stand up and face troubles, conflicts, trials, and tribulations—that these are inevitable in society. They do not delegate to others or set performance standards.

Coddlers wince at the whinings of others. They do not require subordinates to give an accounting for their performance. Coddlers are afraid to provide needed feedback to folks who are not "making it." They patronize endless training programs and fabricate sinecures for failures, rather than cleaning out deadwood and helping those with potential make new starts along more productive paths.

Hagglers

Want to trade? The haggler sees work as a marketplace for exchanging and dickering over any tidbits of value. Relationships, information, ideas, space, and materials are all commodities for the organizational exchange. Hagglers have bits and pieces but never get their hands on the real thing. They are forever out on the street bartering, instead of in the arena where the action is. These corporate scouts work forever on recruiting players, finding bargain-basement equipment, and arranging the lineup. They never get into the real game. In fact, they don't know what the real game is or where it is being played, let alone knowing the score.

Hobblers

Hobblers are the administrative perfectionists. They live and die by the rules. Ask a question and you get chapter and verse on why it can't be done. Success is following procedure—strictly by the book. Printed manuals, regulations, and codes are their articles of faith. Their legalistic-style bible is an indexed, cross-referenced, and leather-bound compendium of officialdom.

Spuddlers

Spuddlers assume airs of importance and make trifles seem significant. They expend their energies on form, not content; on image, not substance. They deal in the shape of the boardroom tables and color of the room, not in the substantive issue and critical decisions. Respect is what they relish, but adulterated adoration is all they get, usually from innocents or other spuddlers who play the same game. They dispense words freely, with pose and flair, but all they convey are clichés.

Spuddlers speak to hear themselves talk, to tickle ears, to fill time. They organize to fill space, then reorganize for self-aggrandizement, to take in more territory. They build empty empires, not profitable domains. Spuddlers sputter when attacked or exposed, ejecting words incoherently, explosively, excitedly to mask the emptiness of their efforts.

Meddlers

Some people can't seem to pass up any organizational "piece of candy." Meddlers hover over, sticking their nose into other people's business, grumbling, darting in and out, dropping a bit of advice, taking the really interesting parts, doing them over, stirring up the pot. But they never accept responsibility for results or for troubles they have created. When promoted, meddlers tinker in work that was formerly theirs; they just can't quite pull themselves away from the technical tasks that were once so satisfying—partly because nobody can do things quite so well as they did.

Meddlers find it easier to criticize, give detailed instructions, and take over than to train and coach. Because of this, their subordinates do not grow in their jobs and develop the mettle needed to succeed. Instead they grow *away* from responsibility, knowing they will not get credit for a job well done—only recrimination for failing to achieve.

Hurdlers

Hurdlers mistake slogans for solutions. They are the dreamers who never touch solid ground and avoid the down-to-earth responsibilities incurred by facing reality. Hurdlers include many do-gooders, social planners, and utopian "medicine men." Often, well-meaning hurdlers do much harm by unrealistically raising expectations or breeding dissatisfaction with more constructive but tedious processes. They issue promises freely, then lament about the performance of others. Hurdlers somehow fail to make clear that such achievements as they espouse require leaping tall buildings at single bounds.

Cobblers

Cobblers are the empiricists, the believers in the machinery of the formal organization. The cobbler esteems the basic organizational hardware and persistently hammers away at minor repairs in the formal organization. The cobbler emphasizes neatness and systems, parceling out territories and "grazing rights." This social engineer methodically pursues measured efficiency in order to crank out the goods—like clockwork, with precision.

Cobblers are dedicated to finding the "one best way" to build organizational structures. They are perennially reorganizing, studying, evaluating, and reassembling new and better systems and gadgets. They work to get it right once and for all, to achieve the perfect fit between ideal and reality. But they fail because people's thoughts and actions cannot be molded to someone else's views, especially when those views embrace a legal-official structure that ignores human needs.

Toddlers

Many organizational workers suffer from the naiveté engendered by extensive miseducation and mistraining. Toddlers do not understand what is going on in the formal or informal organization. Often they are cry babies, frightened by the glare of realities they fail to comprehend and accept. With growing denial and cynicism, they soon—and sometimes repeatedly—pick up their toys and leave with a pout, expecting the professional playpen to be more hospitable elsewhere.

Employers are prone to perpetuate the problem,

tossing toddlers untimely sink-or-swim challenges to test their potential or extending endlessly the internships, trainee programs, and rites of passage. Generally, what toddlers really need is an initial diet of guidance, followed by reality coaching, modeling, feedback, graduated responsibility, and accountability for results.

Fumblers

Fumblers are perpetually vulnerable and always seem to be getting clobbered. They are shaken up, slow to recover, and out of play. Fumblers lack peripheral vision and foresight. Unable to see what's coming, they fail to take precautionary measures to protect themselves. They often make startling starts but end up getting gunned down, fading, or dropping the ball.

Fumblers have a game plan, but it's borrowed from someone else. Not knowing the plan intuitively—by "owning" the plan—they must stop to think when challenged. That's when achievement passes them by. They can't adjust spontaneously, instantaneously, second-naturedly. Then comes the crunch. Hesitation throws off their timing. Fellow workers risk exposure to the consequences of their errors. Fumblers will read this book, agree, try to adjust, work hard, and fail to achieve.

Shuttlers

Shuttlers are on the right track but have not yet arrived. They engage in shuttles, which are, in effect, prehuddles. Shuttles are the place where the huddling groundwork is laid: participants are "friend-

shipped" and "fellowshipped" into the huddling
network. Shuttlers work on building understanding
and trust, sometimes to repair breaches in relations. It
is here that values, attitudes, personalities, skills,
knowledge, and potential contributions are surveyed
and assessed, often through seeming small talk.
Idiosyncrasies and working styles are scrutinized. Participants evaluate possible working arrangements.

Shuttlers are often seeking to gain increased visibility and to project a favorable image so they can
contribute more meaningfully. They are seeking not
only to sell themselves but to find others. It is here
that potential contributors become true huddlers and
nonrelationships grow into huddling associations. The
shuttle gets people from wherever they are to where
huddling can begin and move forward. Shuttles are
the passageway to constructive roles, the umbilical
cord to productivity.

This brief examination of what huddling *is not*
should help clarify what huddling is. *Huddling is a
positive, results-oriented, working relationship between people who are trying to be productive.* Huddles are not self-serving or ends in themselves. They
provide the much needed kinetic energy for the organization. Where the official organization fails, huddles get results.

Huddlers are engaged in a craft, responsibly applying management techniques and know-how; building on experiences and new ideas to get a job done;
sharing insights and observations to help others contribute and grow; keeping alive the most responsive
work ethic in our complex organizational society.

5
Huddling Harbingers

NOTHING comes from nothing. "We see farther by standing on the shoulders of giants" is a truism verified by history. My ideas about huddling did not come from nothing. They emerged from my varied experiences and observations, from my trials and successes in managing and coaching business leaders, and from bits and pieces of professional literature, personal research, and daily news accounts of how people manage to do things.

Every subject has literary "harbingers"—earlier works that sow the seeds for the new ideas to grow. All the writings discussed in this chapter have had some influence on my ideas about huddling, although I must admit I cannot attribute huddling theory to any one of them.

Some of the writings illustrate the "hard-nosed" views of organizational structure and management. Other literature focuses on the human dimensions of organizations and lays more direct groundwork for huddling theory. My purpose in taking you through this brief literary excursion is to increase your insight and confidence in (1) the reality of the formal and informal dimensions of organizations, and (2) the validity of the huddling processes and techniques described in this book.

Political Intrigue

Several management writings have drawn from the medieval writer Niccolò Machiavelli, a keen observer of political processes in his day and an adviser to reigning powers. Elements of huddling can be found in a number of his conclusions, although huddling is not wholly a political process. A few paraphrased ideas will illustrate his approach:

1. Prudence requires checking risks, attitudes, and proven paths.
2. Get the bad over with; dribble out benefits, not bad news or negative deeds.
3. A leader imposed on the people is harder to sustain than one chosen on the basis of popular support.
4. Avoid mercenaries. Build allegiances that transcend money.
5. Be frugal. A person without resources has no power.
6. Seek respect rather than love.
7. Minimize the risks you take. When you do put yourself behind something, commit yourself to

the extent of the loss you may suffer or the gain
you may achieve.

8. Indecisiveness hurts everyone.

9. Don't reach too far. Watch out for greed and
overcommitment.

Machiavelli's writings offer considerable wisdom
for huddlers, though they must be sifted carefully for
ideas that readily apply.

Superintending

In the mid-1800s the Industrial Revolution
changed the old ways of working. Some businesses
adopted operating strategies that allowed them to
grow into giants. National firms were a new phenomenon, girded by new technologies, transportation systems, marketing procedures, and other practices.
These companies could no longer be overseen personally by the owner or general manager. New concepts of management were required.

During this period Daniel C. McCallum was general superintendent of the Erie Railroad, the largest in
the United States. His six principles of general administration are typical of the nineteenth-century approach to creating manageable *formal* organizational
structures. Since that time, virtually all formalized
management ideas—flown under numerous and assorted banners—have emphasized control over the organization through legal and mechanical means.

McCallum's principles of management emphasize
the following:

1. A proper division of work and responsibilities
among employees.

2. Sufficient formal authority to enable responsibilities to be carried out.
3. A means of knowing whether responsibilities assigned are carried out and completed.
4. Prompt reporting and correction of poor performance in duties.
5. Daily reports and follow-up checks, made impersonally so as not to embarrass officers or lessen their influence with subordinates.

With this type of thinking it was natural for organizations to develop along two lines: (1) the creation of carefully engineered legal structures and control systems and, (2) the development, in reaction, of informal patterns of operation that we can now see clearly as huddling.

Bureaucracy

All large organizations—in industry, education, and government—are bureaucracies. Max Weber, a social theorist in the nineteenth century, wrote a treatise on bureaucracy that described with great insight how complex organizations ought to be managed. Weber described bureaucracies in formal terms as having the following attributes:

1. Official business is conducted continuously over time, not intermittently.
2. Business is conducted in accordance with formal, written rules.
3. Official responsibility and authority exist in a hierarchy. Higher officers supervise lower officers.
4. Officers and other employees do not necessar-

ily own the resources used in the performance
of their duties. But they are accountable for
how they use these resources.

5. Offices are occupied temporarily by individuals and are not private property that can be
sold or inherited.
6. Official business is transacted through extensive use of written documents.
7. Officers are appointed to their positions on a
contractual basis.
8. Employees exercise only the authority delegated to them through impersonal rules that
apply generally.
9. Employers are appointed to jobs and given assignments on the basis of their technical qual-
ifications.
10. Officers are compensated through a salary—
regular set payments. They progress through
regular advancements that follow a lifetime
career pattern.

Weber's ideas contrast markedly with the concepts
of huddling we have examined thus far. Still, his
views about bureaucracies and industrial management have a strong bearing on people's thinking today. Most large companies are officially organized as
bureaucracies. But, as we know, many people don't
operate that way.

Time and Motion

Another set of management techniques swept into
play in the twentieth century. The basic thought was
this: *one best way can be found for doing every job.*
The proponent of this theory was an engineer named
Frederick Winslow Taylor. Taylor and his disciples

saw the need for planning, organizing, and controlling. They preached that the objective of good management was to pay high wages and have low unit production costs. Workers were to be rewarded financially according to their output.

Taylor's ideas about management can be summarized as follows:

1. Develop a set of scientifically determined procedures for each segment of a person's work. These are to replace individualized, off-the-cuff methods used by workers.
2. Select and train each worker according to scientific principles, instead of allowing workers to select their own jobs and train themselves as best they can.
3. Supervise the work and follow up to ensure that it is being done according to the scientific principles developed.

Many other ramifications are evident from Taylor's writings. However, these limited concepts illustrate the emphasis given in formal organizations to structuring work and trying to fit workers into a "machinelike" pattern through training and reward systems.

There is, of course, nothing wrong with efficiency as such. But it is this type of lock-step, rigid thinking—particularly when applied to professional, administrative, or managerial jobs—that leads some people to huddling as a workable alternative.

Human Relations

Elton Mayo and his associates opened management's eyes to the social dimensions of the organization. They concluded that scientific, rational principles were not the sole determinants of productivity. Psychological and social factors also had considerable influence on the functioning of organizations. Mayo and others demonstrated that:

1. Organizations have a culture of their own.
2. Workers must be satisfied with their work in order to be motivated.
3. The authority of managers must be won. It is granted only to the extent that subordinates follow.
4. Norms and standards of performance develop among work groups and influence the behavior of all members.

Huddling theory benefits from a number of ideas embedded in the behavioral work of Mayo. Huddling is part of the culture of all organizations. Studies by Homans, Lewin, Selznick, and others have amply documented the influence of informal, social conditions on organizational work.

Management by Objectives

Various modern authors have expounded on the importance of working *purposefully*. Peter Drucker is the foremost proponent of what is popularly called management by objectives (MBO). Drucker and others have presented a number of convincing ideas:

1. Work activities are best organized around purposes or objectives to be achieved.
2. Structure and systems for organizing and managing are appropriate only to the extent that

they further the accomplishment of objectives.

3. Executives should devote their time to those activities that contribute to organizational objectives.

4. The proportion of "knowledge workers" is increasing in comparison with "physical workers." Thus more attention must be given to the organization of creativity and mental processes within bureaucratic settings.

5. Organizations should support meaningful contributions by people, not mere activities.

You can see very well the differences between this type of thinking and more structural approaches. Huddling is purposeful and results-oriented. It incorporates the *intent* of MBO. But many MBO "programs" are ineffective because of their overemphasis on structures, procedures, and reports.

Other Concepts

Many other authors and ideas have influenced huddling theory. It is impossible here to make a thorough review of the literature, but there are a few more writers who are hard to ignore:

Chester I. Barnard, a former president of New Jersey Bell, asserts that effective authority in organizations is generated from the bottom up, not imposed on people from the top down. It is the followers who grant authority to the leader—by following. We all know the impact that legal authority can have on an action, but Barnard adds the important idea that authority comes from several sources.

Rensis Likert describes a process of interlocking activities and memberships in organizations. A super-

visor works with her team of subordinates. She also
represents that group as a member in her boss's team
of subordinates. This creates a "linking pin" effect
throughout the organization, a network of associations.
The notion of huddle networks and interlocking "in-
clusions" has direct relationships to Likert's excellent
concepts.

Richard E. Neustadt, in his writings on presidential power, proposes the concept of "idiosyncratic
credit": those reserves of power and goodwill to be
drawn upon and spent by leaders. These power reserves are replenished by favors and services
rendered—stockpiling goodwill through various
means. In other words, power does not come solely
from legal rights and delegated authority.

Theory X and Theory Y make a powerful contribution by Douglas McGregor. He says, in short, that our
assumptions—biases and theories we carry around in
our heads—guide our actions in organizational work.
If we believe people are lazy and irresponsible
(Theory X), we will tighten controls and structure
work more precisely. If we assume people are intelligent and responsible and can be self-motivated
(Theory Y), we will approach others in the organization with more trust and freedom. The attitudes toward other people and assumptions about work that
underlie huddling activities parallel McGregor's
Theory Y.

J. Sterling Livingston downplays the role of formal
education in managerial work, emphasizing instead
the need to select managers who have a natural gift for
leading and for "finding opportunities." Livingston
stresses the importance of experience and feedback in
the growth of organizational workers. Huddling provides some clues about how these forces operate and
might better be harnessed.

Laurence J. Peter (*Peter Principle*) presents the intriguing notion that people rise in organizations until they reach their level of incompetence. So long as people succeed in their work, they keep getting promoted. When they fail, they are stuck in a job they can't handle and usually are not moved out. Thus, after a while, organizations are filled with incompetents. Huddling occurs to compensate for this problem, to the extent that it exists in an organization.

Organization development (OD), another contemporary idea, emphasizes the need to build a more favorable atmosphere for interpersonal relations and work activities. This atmosphere can be created by fostering trust, openness, feedback, and humane exchanges of ideas and influence. Obviously, some climates are more supportive of huddling than others. In some organizations the risk of venturing stultifies initiative and problem solving. OD could help to create a more favorable climate for the operation of both the formal and informal organization.

6
Huddle Blindness

*I*T was a frustrating situation for George. He was president of a small firm in a high-growth business and had visions of becoming the IBM of the industry. His products and services were excellent, but they didn't sell well. Staff turnover was high. Bickering was up and morale was down. In an attempt to surmount these problems, George spent much of the time in his secluded, spacious office refiguring prices and costs, retooling services and delivery systems, changing job descriptions, and redrawing the organization chart. Finally he hired an independent consultant, an older man he respected. George was furious when the consultant said that he was his own problem. George simply didn't understand how to work with people— either his employees or his customers.

George's problem was huddle blindness: he did not understand the huddling process and how to use it effectively. His lack of insight and skill led him into nonhuddler roles, as it will any organizational worker. In undertaking huddling responsibilities you must make sure to distinguish those who can operate under informal leadership and working arrangements from those who by nature work "by the book." If a job cannot be done adequately with the official organization, and requires huddling capability, it would be calamitous to place somebody in charge who does not understand huddling. This chapter provides a checklist to help you assess yourself and others for true huddling capabilities.

Formality

When looking for someone to fill a key huddling assignment, ask yourself: Does the person think that significant decisions always require holding formal meetings? Is the person hung up with using Robert's Rules of Order or some other formal system for conducting meetings? How about the use of formal names and titles?

Does the person rely too much on formal communications through briefings, written reports, and structured meetings? This is not to suggest that formal mechanisms aren't important. But if people do not understand that formal communications have a right time and place and fail to appreciate the value of informal communications, they will not function well in huddles. This is true in government as well as in industry. Effective workers "grease the skids" through informal contacts so that the decision is made before the formal decision-making process begins.

Helmut Knipp, general manager of the Capitol Hilton, maintains that the essence of commerce is people—people working with people in acceptable surroundings. He disdains the formidable desk, constant interruptions, telephone calls, and omnipresent secretary in his business dealings. Instead, he says, "If you can get a person to lunch or dinner, you have the person's undivided attention and can, therefore, much more effectively sell your idea or your product."*

In a similar vein, speaking of business lunches and entertainment, Senator Russell Long said: "Entertainment is to business what fertilizer is to agriculture. It increases the yield." Both these men understand the essence of huddling in their domains.

Organization Charts

True huddlers understand the nature of power. They know that even though significant authority is held by higher-level officials, all power does not reside in the office of top management. If a person tends to be a "true believer" in organizational structure, you should be careful in using him in any significant leadership assignment.

Does the person view the organization chart as defining channels of communication and decision making? Most organizations (and people working in them) would fail if they went strictly by the structure outlined in the chart.

Job Descriptions

What is the person's view of a job description? In more important jobs, it is often unwise to operate

* _The Washington Post_, April 3, 1978.

strictly on the basis of a job description. In order to achieve results, a person must recognize problem areas as well as opportunities and avoid moving indiscreetly into off-limit areas. The person you are looking for in key assignments must intuitively understand the concept of working enclaves (see Chapter 8) and be able to move in and out of assignments, rather than strictly following a job description.

After firing his second research director, one organization head said: "Maybe we were too unclear about what we wanted him to do." In fact, the research director had had a specific, written, legal job description that he tried diligently to follow. The boss was not satisfied; he felt that the "real" job was not being handled satisfactorily. The research director didn't know the difference between a job description and the needs and expectations of others, and the organization head failed to take into account the formal duties that the director was trying to carry out.

Work Plans

What is the person's view of work plans and organizational objectives? Work planning and MBO systems have many merits, but anyone receiving a key management or leadership assignment must recognize that priorities change and that work activities must shift to meet rising demands. Formal objectives cannot always be ignored, and an ability to report favorably on the progress of formal work plans and organizational objectives may be quite important.

Fights

Does the person know the difference between fighting and working strategically? Many workers cannot distinguish a hassle from a huddle. Hassles generate heat and perpetuate the ruckus. Huddles get things going and clear away obstacles between personalities and goals.

For many people, confusion is the major by-product of any formal organizational effort. Huddles clear up this confusion and allow relationships to be defined, complaints to be heard, adjustments to be made, legitimate credit to be given when due, encouragement to be shared, and flags of warning to be raised.

Compensation

What is the person's view of financial rewards? Because contributions through the informal organization are not directly correlated to the formal organization, there will always be some inequity in financial rewards or recognition through formal status and position. However, leaders must recognize that justice tends to come in the long run rather than in the short run. Therefore, excessive concern about immediate rewards will be detrimental to accomplishing the work of the organization.

Effective leaders know that money is not the only—or even the best—carrot for organizational productivity. Employees do not work for money alone. Psychological reward is important too. Huddles are voluntary activities and thrive on psychic compensation.

Hierarchy

What is the person's view of top management? Many people believe that top executives know more than anyone else about what is going on—that they have a good handle on organizational realities. Effective huddlers realize that many people in official positions, no matter how high their status, are blocked off from essential information and often have a distorted view of what is going on in their area of responsibility. Huddling compensates for gaps in information and understanding on the part of executives at all levels in the organization.

Documents

What is the person's view of formal documents and records? Huddling activities are not documented except in the participants' minds or perhaps in a few scribbled notations. The true findings of a formal organizational study may be better represented by discussions in huddles than by an official report. Effective huddlers realize that it is sometimes wiser to communicate through certain informal information channels rather than through formal reports or public disclosures. The functional value of huddles becomes apparent in this type of circumstance.

Politics

Is the person intolerant of the way things *really* work? Is the person upset by huddling—by what appear to be "end runs," insubordination, lack of respect, and "deviousness"? If people cannot tolerate disorder and work within it, they will not work well in huddles.

For generations some people have functioned effectively in informal organizations through huddling.

Such people readily adapt themselves to huddling in order to get things done. But the vast majority of workers do not understand how things really get done, nor are they tolerant of the huddling process. The more people who understand how to get results through huddling, the more effective the organization.

II
Huddling Strategy

TRADITIONAL management theories and organizational systems do not help workers get a handle on informal organizations and huddling processes. Huddlers need to understand the realities of organizational life—unofficial and official—so they can adjust their approach to make things work better. These organizational realities form the basis of huddling strategy.

7
Assertive Authority

HIS name is almost never mentioned in talk about who's who in the company. In fact, anyone trying to place him in the pecking order would have to search the organization chart carefully to find him. This hasn't stopped him from quietly assuming a growing role in the company since it was acquired by the new parent corporation. He is, in practice, second in command and able to wield considerable influence. The new owners have talked of making his position "official" but feel that things need to settle down a bit more first. A few people are aware of the personal relationship he has with the new chairman and the esteem in which he is held. Those who have worked with him have no doubt about his self-confidence, skill, and ability to get things done.

Above, a thumbnail sketch of the skillful huddler—the results-oriented leader who knows the value of assertive authority in the informal organization. *Assertive authority is the power and influence enjoyed by huddlers who assume a dynamic posture, take the initiative, get involved in the action, and cause something to happen.*

Traditional authority conferred by the formal organization—based on position, legal rights, and status—has only a limited bearing on the informal organization. This is not to say that position and status play no role in the informal organization. Typically, however, power and authority within a huddle come from other sources—primarily from the ability to contribute meaningfully and skillfully to the solution of problems. In a sense, effective huddlers carry their rank in their person, not in their job. Huddling creates an unparalleled demand for competence. Without productive contributions in the informal organization, assertive authority does not exist.

Inner Resources

In the huddle an ability to contribute and exercise authority comes from expertise, reputation from past deeds, strength of relationships with others, access to influential people and groups, and the ability to work with the formal organization. But all these have little value unless the huddler has the resources to employ them. For instance, if a huddler has expertise but lacks the ability to deploy it to the advantage of the organization, he cannot be productive.

Reputation for past contributions has a bearing on authority only to the extent that the person can contribute anew and is given an opportunity to do so.

Friendships, working relationships, and access to other influential people are also significant, but only to the extent that they bear on the current situation and can be drawn upon effectively. Similarly, legal rights and formal position can help only if they are related to the current situation and are not going to be checked or nullified by the superior status of an opponent.

Strategic Use of Influence

Another overriding factor in assertive authority is the ability to make strategic use of available sources of influence and power. That is, if you have the roots of power and influence but cannot deliver the goods or effect a needed change, all else is to no avail. The ability to tap the *potential* for such power depends on your ability to "put it all together," to act with proper timing, and to set into motion a sequence of actions that will produce results.

In one company, for example, a new executive took over as chief executive officer, coming in from the outside to rebuild the organization. She brought some of her previous staff with her—men whose loyalty and skill she could depend on. She recognized the strength of her position. People generally were ready for a change. She retired a few executives and moved others around. She established informal working relations with several younger workers who had strong reputations as doers. Her new associates took time to "wine and dine" staff and managers. They did the same with labor leaders.

Through these and other well-timed actions, the new CEO broke up several old huddling relationships, instituted strong new ones topside, forged a strong network of huddles she could influence, and wisely saved herself for those critical huddles that would keep her in touch and on top of matters. In effect, she deftly used the resources at her disposal— official and unofficial—to place herself in the best possible position to carry out her duties and to achieve the goals to which she had committed herself and her associates.

Self-Confidence

Assertive authority depends on the self-confidence of the huddler and his ability to communicate that self-confidence to others. The *person* is the primary instrument of power in the informal organization. Self-confidence and timing are the backbone of power once an appropriate strategy has been formulated. The greatest of plans are to no avail if the creator of those plans does not believe in the creator of those plans. Confidence is the foundation of assertiveness, and assertiveness is what makes huddling work. Huddlers do not flourish on humble pie, apologies for ineptness, doormatlike stances, or mellowness. Cockiness is out, however; reasonable, well-placed self-confidence is in and necessary.

Knowledge of Territories

The appropriateness of a huddler's strategy and the degree of self-confidence are relative matters. Confidence usually varies with the nature of the situation. The appropriateness of a stragegy must be measured against the moves of others.

The environment within which a strategy is employed is normally a "moving target." As new individuals come on the scene, as the mix of problems, issues, and circumstances changes, and as your credibility is tested, you must repeatedly reassess your power base. Strategic planning and the assessment of your ability to assert authority are a continuing process.

Assertive authority depends on knowing the territory involved—the needs of others, the problems faced, and the issues to be dealt with. Effective huddlers know the extent and sources of the power possessed by others. They know their own strengths and weaknesses and are able to make reasonably accurate assessments of the risks involved in undertaking certain actions. Huddles are a vital place for picking up knowledge of the territory being worked and for testing prior knowledge. Certification for being "streetwise" is granted in the huddling milieu.

Win-Win Attitude

As you deal with others in a huddle, your long-term (and in most cases short-term) effectiveness depends on your willingness to be honest and fair with those around you. Authority is asserted only through other people, and in most cases results can be achieved only through their cooperation and participation.

To be an effective huddler, you must take actions that avoid bringing about unnecessary losses for others. Whenever possible you should explore win-win possibilities for all parties involved. That is, you should plan and act so that whenever possible other people get something and no one is hurt. People do not always have to get what they want, but they should be treated humanely and with respect.

Checks on Authority

Assertive authority is exercised within certain boundaries. To begin with, it is likely to be checked to a degree by the *assertive authority of someone else* or by the *legitimate authority* of the formal organization. Because of this, in only a very few circumstances will a radical or revolutionary change be successful. You must have endless patience and endurance to get results in such a complex setting.

Assertive authority is also checked by the *rules of the game*—the bounds of permissible action in the informal organization. Be aware of taboos, legal restrictions, precedents to be respected, feelings to be honored, territorial rights of others, customs, courtesies, and any other constraints or imperatives. These will vary from place to place and group to group, and will undoubtedly evolve over time. They are part of the glue that holds the jumble of informal activities together. They are the circumspect behaviors expected of those allowed into the realm of leadership.

Knowing how to get around the organization without being out of bounds, unethical, or unworthy of responsibility and trust is an essential part of assertive authority. However, recognize that the rules of the game sometimes need to be changed and should become the target of responsible huddling activities.

Unstuck Solutions

Keep in mind that assertive authority is likely to have only temporary results. That is, *most problems do not stay solved.* Many solutions end up unsolving something else and creating new problems. In addition, since most huddling activities take place within the dynamic arena of competing forces and interests, one exercise of influence may trigger another and may even set the problem back to its unresolved state. This is why, once an action is set in motion by the informal organization, it is often advisable to reinforce it with subsequent actions by the formal organization.

In essence, assertive authority in the informal organization is functional authority. It is based on the pragmatic idea that *if you can cause something to happen, you have power.* Assertive authority is the ability to persuade, direct, convince, entice, and induce others to act in a way that will bring about changes, smooth ruffled feathers, transfer information, promote new perceptions and outlooks, and reinforce values. It is the ability to contribute to the well-being of the organization through improving working environments and furthering organizational goals.

8
Working Enclaves

K AY was hired to type, file, take dictation, keep time cards, open correspondence, answer the phone, and record minutes of staff meetings. She does all these things. But while others go out to lunch she, the branch manager, and his assistant often get together informally and talk. Usually they end up discussing business matters such as tough loan applications, bad loans, problem employees, and office practices. This is where most of the office management decisions are made. Because of Kay's insights and good judgment, her opinions on all these matters carry considerable weight.

As this example shows, huddlers exercise influence within a specific domain or territory. This sphere of influence is called a *working enclave*. Normally, the working enclave does not correspond exactly to the huddler's job description. The job description designates an area of responsibility within the formal organization, but it does not necessarily define the area in which the person is working.

Many people who have a clear and precise job description still have no idea of what they are supposed to be doing. Other people can operate influentially without any official position. Woodrow Wilson's wife reportedly ran the government during the President's illness. Rosalynn Carter became one of President Carter's closest advisers, as did Charles Kirbo of Atlanta, a lawyer with no formal position in the administration.

Opportunity

The working enclave often is created from the interests of the huddler and the person assertively moving into various areas of activity. A person can also be drawn informally into enclaves that are not primary areas of interest. For instance, a problem emerges in the office and needs to be handled immediately. Those responsible do not stop and check job descriptions. They reach out and find someone who *can contribute* to resolving the problem, someone who is willing to get involved.

Not uncommonly, a formally established position, with written duties and responsibilities, will have as its real purpose freeing someone to participate in huddling situations on behalf of higher-level management. This is often the nature, in part, of the assistant-to position: a person moves into an area under another's supervision to get results where the formal supervisor cannot.

Responsibility

Numerous leadership gaps exist in any organization. These gaps are filled by huddlers who have a sense of responsibility. Huddlers get involved in an area outside their formal duties because something must be done to correct a situation or to stave off a potentially troublesome problem for the organization.

Sometimes people get drawn into unofficial responsibilities by official means. An individual may be assigned "on detail" to a task force or some other unusual duty. A person may be asked unofficially to sit in on certain meetings to "keep in touch" with a part of the organization or simply to function as an emissary with certain groups and keep abreast of what is going on. Such entry into new working areas may be quite subtle and may go unrecognized by others. Or it may be overt, with an official announcement that the person will spend some time in new areas of responsibility.

Incompleteness and Incompetence

People often get involved in activities outside their official spheres because of the incompleteness of job descriptions. Areas of responsibility are not thoroughly defined and gaps exist in the definition of work and tasks to be done. Therefore, individuals may see a need to act unofficially to take care of matters.

Most job descriptions are obsolete. So are most manuals and instructions. They may have been adequate at one time, but because of changes they no longer meet the demands of the organization. It becomes imperative, therefore, for huddlers to see what needs to be done, take the initiative, and meet current and future needs according to real priorities.

Huddlers also get involved in unofficial responsibilities because of the nonperformance of others. Many people are either incompetent or otherwise unable to do what they are supposed to do. Huddlers must complete those assignments whenever possible. Incompetence is a major problem in most organizations. It can be reduced through better screening techniques for job candidates in management and other responsible positions and through improved training and coaching.

Interests and Ambitions

People who are dissatisfied with their official areas of work naturally seek assignments in areas of greater interest. They reach out and do tasks that are interesting and challenging, and by so doing move into the territory of others or into vacuums where some contribution is needed.

Other people may well be happy with their official assignments but still feel a need to do more. They reach out because they simply can't sit back and see problems go unresolved. They are curious and aggressive, often driven by psychological needs they don't fully understand.

Still other people are drawn into new areas because of their strong ambitions. They drive themselves to assume authority, to exercise influence over others, and to enlarge their spheres of responsibility. Often they get involved and make significant contributions in order to be given even more responsibility. These ambitious huddlers have a *constructive* need to exercise power. They are not to be confused with hustlers, who seek status, power, and reward without regard to the welfare of the organization.

Networks

Working enclaves are not restricted to areas of direct involvement and personal interest. They can also extend to secondary huddles in which the huddler exercises influence but does not participate directly. This occurs through *networks,* or interlocking huddles. For instance, you may be included in several huddles with people who are involved in additional huddles. This provides an informal chain of huddles through which activities and actions are unofficially coordinated.

Huddling networks build out in various directions. They go up, down, across, and diagonally throughout the organization. Sometimes they follow official organization lines; at other times they skip around seemingly at random. Sue, the president, confers with Joe, the general manager, and Alex, a supply clerk; Joe takes the matter up with his foremen and the time clerk; Alex checks with one of the production supervisors; and on and on.

Huddle networks also spread outside the official organization to involve families, competitors, suppliers, buyers, governments. Huddlers who recognize these patterns are able to reach out in various directions to get things done.

Identifying Enclaves

How do you identify working enclaves? Since they do not exist on the organization chart and are not documented in the records, you will have to use other methods of identification. One is by *asking:* "Who works with whom?" "Who handles certain kinds of problems?" People may not be fully aware of the working enclaves around them, but the proper questions can help you get the information you need. You can find out who was present when a certain matter was discussed in so-and-so's office, or who came up with certain facts or gave the go-ahead on a project.

Working enclaves can also be identified by *watching*. Observe who talks to whom, where people go for decisions. Look closely at huddles, even if what is being said or what is taking place is not immediately apparent. With careful observation you should be able to assess some of the activities occurring in those huddles. This method is limited, of course, because much of huddling is hidden from the view of those who are not directly involved. But as someone said: "You can see a lot by watching."

A third approach is a more scientific one—the *sociometric method*. This constitutes a systematic study, by structured observation and interview, of who participates in different kinds of problems, who talks to whom, who leads, who follows, and what the nature of the groupings is. This method has been used in small-group research and in organization and community studies.

9
Affirmative Control

S OME actions produce results that are greater than the sum of their parts. That is, more comes out than was put in. Control within huddles is generally of this nature: expansive rather than constricting, inducing rather than threatening. This type of control involves an active release of internal energies, a channeling or harnessing of desired actions and a restraining of undesired actions. *Affirmative control is the positive regulation of action so as to provide leadership in complex social situations.*

Since the contributions of huddling are unofficial, normal means of reward and punishment are not available. One of the significant challenges for leaders is to motivate those who are contributing in the informal organization but who are not getting equitable rewards through the formal organization. It is very frustrating for people to make significant contributions without being given status or monetary compensation in accordance with their true worth. Patience and restraint are demanded at that point, or else people's dissatisfaction will begin to undermine their usefulness.

Formal Rewards

Formal rewards are of several types. Money is one of the most common. According to many people, those who contribute the most should be paid more. But if an individual's greatest contributions are made in the informal organization, it is often difficult to provide fair pay.

Status is another formal reward—giving a person a higher position in technical, management, or staff functions. However, if a person who makes important contributions is a lower-level employee, it is difficult to jump him over several hierarchal levels to a position equal in status to what he has achieved in the informal organization.

Honors and recognition are other formal rewards. Sometimes honors commensurate with a person's contribution to huddles are not in order. For example, if the person works behind the scenes to cover up for a serious breach in the organization or the failure of a key individual, it may be impossible to fully recognize his contribution. To do so would undermine the official, formal organization.

People are also rewarded on an official basis by corner offices, larger desks, rugs on the floor, and private bathrooms. While such rewards could also be given to prized contributors in the informal organization, if they are too conspicuous and in open conflict with the formal organization they will be detrimental to the overall operation of the organization. For instance, a company vice-president may not be performing his official duties satisfactorily. If lower-level individuals take over his leadership functions, it would be difficult to give them bigger offices and other trappings of status greater than those of the executive they officially report to. It would probably also undermine the effectiveness of the lower-level officials. In any "shoot out" in the official organization, they may well lose out.

One of the biggest limitations of formal rewards is that they do not always reveal how well a person is doing. Sometimes a person is given a reward by the formal organization (such as a pay raise or promotion) as compensation for not being included in significant events in the informal organization.

For example, a faithful employee who has served for years in important assignments may fail to adjust to changes in corporate strategy, a new crowd in power, or shifts in external conditions. The organization may need to get this employee out of the way so that the organization can function more effectively. Such a person may be given a raise and "kicked upstairs"— promoted into a senior staff position or an innocuous vice-presidency. Despite the conspicuous reward from the formal organization, the person may in fact be getting the ax, ostracized from the informal organization so that effective work can go on.

Informal Incentives

The difficulty of rewarding contributors in the informal organization underscores the importance of affirmative control. Huddling provides a way of partially rewarding the real contributors in an organization by building on their interests and natural drives. These rewards are internal, nonbankable; often they yield monetary payoffs only in the long run. For many contributors, a good deal of the reward comes from the results attained.

The formal organization can legally bind employees to perform certain duties. The informal organization has no such legal charter. Work in the informal organization is voluntary: *huddlers are volunteers.* As a result, some informal reward structure is needed to motivate workers to contribute to the unofficial organization.

Affirmative control enables those who exercise leadership to tap the interests and needs of huddle participants. Indeed, the only real source of control in the informal organization comes from harnessing the "energy" produced by people's interests and commitments. This energy can be tapped by initiating huddling activities with others or offering them new challenges and opportunities.

Affirmative control does not mean an absence of orders and commands. However, if commands from the formal organization become dominant, they will be ineffective, because they fail to meet the needs and drives of participants. The influence of the formal organization will be eroded. Affirmative control represents the most viable strategy for tapping the energy needed to make things happen.

Tapping interests. Huddlers differ in their interests and drives. Some are naturally drawn to planning overall strategy, being involved in the big picture. Others are turned on by laying out a plan or putting meat on a strategic "skeleton." Still others want to carry out a plan that has already been formulated.

Some people are better as "up front" problem

identifiers; others are more effective as trou-
bleshooters after the problem has been defined. Some
individuals enjoy paperwork, while others prefer action and results. The challenge in the informal organization is to understand the unique interests and motivations of people so they can be directed toward the
assignments to be accomplished.

Keep in mind that some people do not look to their
work to satisfy their basic interests. They want their
paychecks but find their rewards and satisfactions
elsewhere—in community and church activities, professional associations, sports, or family relationships.
Often, they are less inclined to get involved in extensive huddling commitments than are those whose
work is their life.

Tapping needs. Huddlers also differ in their needs.
Those with a high need for achievement seek out and
welcome challenging opportunities. They are risk
takers and like to be involved in projects where immediate feedback is available. Such people show a lot
of initiative and often get involved in developing new
business ventures and challenging projects.

People with a high need for affiliation prefer the
support that comes from interaction with other individuals. Those with a high power drive need to exercise influence and control over others. They are usually willing to knock heads together and handle troublesome people problems. By understanding the different needs and motives of the people you work with,
you can better influence what is happening through
affirmative control.

Positive and Negative Controls

Control in huddles can be employed in negative as
well as positive ways. Negative controls include sub-

tly phasing out unproductive people, gradually taking over their areas of contribution, or cutting them off from important sources of communication. All these actions take away people's motivation. Threats and reprisals from the informal organization are also effective. For instance, a person may be given a promotion by the formal organization but told behind closed doors that he has a certain amount of time to find another job.

Positive controls consist of giving people challenging opportunities to perform, getting them into meaningful work, tapping their talents and hidden potential, and providing social and psychological payoffs.

Satisfaction comes from seeing that one has an important contribution to make and being able to do so. Individuals who make needed contributions are usually more motivated and committed than those who are involved in menial tasks. This does not mean that only "big" and exciting responsibilities are motivating. A small but significant task or minor project detail can make people feel that they are contributing meaningfully to the informal organization.

It should be clear that people need to be paid for their work and given status and formal positions as consistent with the job they do as possible. But this is often difficult when people's contributions are part of the unofficial organization. Affirmative control helps leaders overcome weaknesses of the formal organization, reward huddlers who contribute, and shape the character of the informal organization. By understanding the concepts and processes described in this chapter, you will be better able to work with the informal organization and make use of affirmative control.

III
Huddling Tactics

IT is one thing to know that huddles exist and that huddling is an ongoing activity in organizations. It is quite another to be able to participate in huddles and make them work for the organization. This section examines ways to become a more effective participant in huddling processes. In effect, it lays the groundrules for successful huddling.

10
Huddle Territory

EFFECTIVE huddling begins with understanding the realities of organizational life. Some people feel that any basically intelligent person, trained in management theories and techniques, will be able to function effectively as a manager in almost any kind of organization. Those who support such a notion of "management generalists" sometimes fail to understand that the foundation of leadership is the ability to understand the specific environment in which the manager must work.

Leadership does not arise from theories and techniques alone. Accurate understanding of a variety of organizational realities is the foundation of effective huddling. These realities should be considered by all institutions involved in preparing managers—schools of business management, public administration, edu-

cational administration, and so forth. Management
specialists as well as generalists must be given this
understanding.

Personalities

Contributors to the informal organization must understand the character of the participants—what
makes them tick. This includes the dominant
personalities—those who are conspicuous, who wield
significant power, and who use their influence to do
the work of the organization. It also includes people
who are less conspicuous and influential. Often they
are tucked away in the organization and can be found
only by questioning, observation, and trial and error.
Some may end up being supply clerks, mail room
clerks, assistant-to's, secretaries, or administrative
support personnel. They may control such things as
petty cash, travel, contracts, conference room scheduling, maintenance, public relations, file storage, data
hardware, executive appointment books, budgets, and
reports.

Unless you comprehend the needs, drives, working styles, strengths, and weaknesses of all these individuals, you will find stumbling blocks in your efforts
to be an effective contributor. Huddles are intimate
encounters between people. You have to know
names—first names, nicknames. You must be aware of
likes, dislikes, foibles, biases, and friendships as you
work with others to carry out common business interests.

Official Rules

Workers need to understand the rules, regulations,
and procedural constraints of the formal organization
in order to operate effectively in the informal organi-

zation. The legality of the formal organization is a reality of working life. If you depart from its prescribed rules or violate its prohibitions, you must be prepared for the consequences.

Sometimes, of course, deviation from official rules is necessary to get things done. But in order to argue for change, you must know what currently exists. In any organization change is as much a matter of moving away from an undesirable situation as it is moving toward an established goal. Therefore, astute participants in the huddling process will use the official rules of the organization not only as guidelines for staying out of trouble but also to further the interests of the informal organization.

Premises

Huddlers must also understand the premises that govern communications and decisions in the informal organization. These are the givens of organizational life, the "mores" of working culture. Often they are unwritten rules of conduct, accepted facts, traditions, or frames of reference with which matters are considered. In many cases they are unwritten and unspoken.

Sometimes unwritten rules conflict with the official rules and procedures of the organization. They may involve such matters as whether production or people come first, rules for promotion and advancement, the proper degree of secretiveness in the organization, and how customers or clients are to be treated. With an understanding of these premises, you will be effective in dealing with those who exercise leadership in the informal organization.

At times it may be necessary, even vital, to change the cultural premises of the organization in order to

keep it viable. Some premises may have become obsolete and may put the organization out of business if
left unchallenged. For instance, in earlier times some
businesses pursued growth through the reinvestment
of earnings rather than by borrowing. With changing
times, that practice became difficult. Those who held
fast to the premise failed to revitalize plants and products and fell behind. Change was essential to growth
and survival, and those who did change were the ones
to grow.

Relationships

To be an effective huddler, you must understand
the network of relationships that exist in the informal
organization. Such knowledge is essential to gain access to huddles, to reach those people who are vital to
your own operations.

People new to organizational life often learn the
value of informal relationships the hard way. During
his campaign, Jimmy Carter repeatedly criticized the
"backslapping, tale-swapping, horse-trading cajolery
of Capitol Hill." * After he took office, he urged his
staff to loosen up and be less aloof, suggesting that
"congresspersons be invited for breakfast or lunch or
to Cabinet members' homes." (Cabinet minutes, February 13, 1978.)

Self-Understanding

An accurate knowledge of your own strengths and
weaknesses is essential to functioning in huddles. You
should know what you can contribute, how you can

* Jack Anderson in *The Washington Post*, March 28, 1978.

best do your work and be most responsible. Often, others will be tolerant of your weaknesses in order to gain the advantages of your strengths. But, you will not be able to protect yourself against criticism and inappropriate assignments unless you understand who you are and what you can do. People are often asked to take on responsibility for a project that goes beyond their drive or skills. Those who understand their own deficiencies will avoid stepping into such failure-prone situations.

By knowing your strengths and recognizing your deficiencies, you will become more confident in the work you do. For instance, if your strength lies in convincing others of ideas and action plans, you can take on responsibilities in those areas with a strong feeling of security. If you are good at details, you can confidently approach assignments that require careful attention or painstaking research.

Organizational Backdrop

The history and environment of the organization are also important to huddlers. You should be aware of what has gone on before: major events, trends, struggles, and past performances. These matters are often recorded in the organization's charter, studies, and reports, as well as in the minds of co-workers.

You should be aware, too, of how your organization fits into its larger environment. Every organization faces outside pressures from government regulatory agencies, competitors, associations, community voices, suppliers, stockholders, legislators, interest groups, bankers, and customers. Within the organization considerable pressure often comes from employee associations or unions. Ignorance of employee contracts or bargaining agreements can get you into trouble. When you are aware of the pressures and the opportunities created by these forces, you will contribute much more effectively as a huddler.

11
Huddling
Relationships

I ONCE counseled a ranking corporate officer who consciously tried to manage on the strength of his interpersonal skills—his ability to relate with people and to build trust and respect. These were things he had read in his management studies, and he was convinced they were right. However, it was obvious to me that he had one major weakness, a flaw that was conspicuous to all those he worked with. His problem was that he aroused people's suspicions. Often he appeared to be manipulative and seemed awkward in dealing with associates when he came out from behind his desk. I was not surprised to learn that he was subsequently passed over for the promotion he expected.

You cannot function as a huddler unless you develop effective working relationships with other people. *Huddles are collegial systems.* You must get yourself into the organizational community. To be standoffish is deadly. It is true that you may be called in to perform a specific task, but unless certain conditions exist or unless you are able to adapt to working with others, you will not be a valued participant in the huddling process. This means that you will be unable to exercise influence and leadership that would otherwise be yours.

People Person

Huddling takes place between two or more people. Some huddlelike activities do occur on an individual level. These consist of pondering, meditating, musing, contemplating, planning, strategizing. However, in order to get around—to get results—you must have contact with people.

I once counseled a manager who was having trouble leading his team of computer specialists. I later videotaped his boss's staff meeting, which involved an hour of problem-solving discussions. The manager never said a word during the meeting. When I quizzed him about his lack of participation, he appeared surprised and claimed to have been actively involved. After reviewing the video replay, he was shocked to realize that his participation was mental rather than interpersonal. He had been right on target with his analyses and perceptions but had failed to convey them to others. While this is an unusual case, it illustrates the importance of active working relationships in contributing meaningfully to huddles.

*You must have contact with people to be a hud-
dler.* Camaraderie is helpful but not essential. You
must be aware of who is around, their interests, needs,
capabilities, and contributions. You cannot isolate
yourself; you must be out among people, where they
are. You must keep in contact with all key figures at all
levels of the organization so that when the need arises
you will be able to take action.

Hubert Humphrey once described how the U.S.
Senate really works: "You've got to know each one of
these people. Some people are no-nonsense. Some
people like a little nonsense. [There's] a lot of cloakroom talk. . . . Now cloakroom talk is like a golfers'
locker room. It's rowdy. It's rough and risqué at times.
Lots of storytelling, laughing, and hootin' and hol-
lerin'. That's when you get to know people." *

Many people view contact with others as ineffi-
cient, messy, and unpleasant. They are easily irritated
by individual idiosyncrasies and weaknesses. Some
are impatient and do not want to get involved in decisions that require convincing co-workers. Others see
involvement as risky, particularly if they have to deal
with other people's problems and emotions.

In order to be successful as a huddler, you must
overcome or at least control feelings of this nature. At
times, you may even have to get involved in parties,
receptions, "bull sessions," and other loci of chatter.
You don't have to be enthusiastic, but you should at
least be tolerant of others and willing to work with
them as best you can.

Telephones

Huddling can occur only when those involved
have a workable relationship. The telephone can be

* *The Washington Post*, October 9, 1977.

an obstruction to huddling if used too early in a relationship. Telephones can hold people at a distance, leaving the conduct of business overly "official." They shut people off from valuable nonverbal messages and inhibit growth of trust.

After a solid working relationship is established, the telephone can provide efficient contacts. It is a useful medium for passing on information or checking its validity, for prodding action, and for showing support or encouragement. Keep in mind, however, that the phone can become a crutch. If relied on too often, it will put you out of face-to-face contact with people, limit your development of new associates, and shield you from the kinds of interactions that get results for the organization. So be aware of both the possibilities and the pitfalls associated with the telephone.

Writings

The same is true for letters, memoranda, and written reports. Don't let these media get in the way of your working relations with people. Particularly, watch your language! Avoid gobbledygook that fails to communicate, stilted, impersonal language that obscures "you" as a huddler, and anything else that delays matter, skirts issues, or allows you to hide from other people associated with the job to be done.

Trust

Trust is an essential element in working with others, particularly in huddles. Feelings of mistrust, suspicions of being under constant attack by others, get in the way of working relationships. This "bunker mentality" was at least partly responsible for the downfall of the Nixon White House. The fear of people and institutions led to defensiveness, counterattack, and overreaction.

In rare cases, mistrust is well founded. But irrational fear and exaggeration of conflicts can be strong deterrents to working relationships. They take up energy that could be used more productively in contributing to the organization. Beware of this type of attitude. Look for the good in others. Give them the benefit of the doubt, but with some degree of caution. Don't invent conflict and danger to escape from engaging in important work with colleagues.

A very talented acquaintance of mine pulled out of an organization in which he had tremendous potential because he felt people were "out to get him." Whenever others criticized him, he interpreted it as a conspiracy. If he didn't get what he wanted, he attributed his failure to the intervention of someone who was trying to do him in. He made himself a loser in that organization and will do so again unless he learns to trust other people.

Trust is a two-way street. You must trust others and be trusted by them. The degree of trust between people varies greatly from huddle to huddle. But in any huddle honesty and openness are essential. This is particularly true when people from different levels in the organization huddle together. In cases involving a boss and subordinate, no fear of entrapment must exist; otherwise the subordinate will withdraw behind the screen of "official" duties and procedures.

When Jimmy Carter took office, he vowed to increase the power of his Cabinet. To promote that power, he selected people with whom he was comfortable; he personally interviewed each one to make sure they could relate on a one-to-one basis. If no rap-

port, no appointment. This established a starting point
for effective huddling.

Predictability

Trust is built on predictability. That is, people
must be able to predict how you will behave under a
given set of circumstances. If you appear erratic and
irregular, you will not be trusted. It is important to
have fairly stable values, personality traits, and approaches to problems and working assignments. This
is not to say that huddlers must be rigid, but rather that
they must be dependable. If others cannot trust you to
do what has to be done, they will begin to look
elsewhere for contributions. People who are always
behind schedule or off target, or who depart from the
unwritten rules of the organization, will not be valued
in the huddling process.

Discretion

Often much of what goes on in huddles is confidential. Those who participate must be assured of
the loyalty and confidentiality of others. People who
talk too much, make disclosures to the wrong people,
or otherwise handle huddling communications indiscreetly will not be tolerated for long. Blind loyalty is
not required, except in rare cases. But discretion and
sound judgment are essential. You must be careful
about what is said, to whom it is said, and the manner
in which such communications occur.

This question of discretion arose in one business
when an officer put some very sensitive information in
memo form. The memo was marked for "limited distribution" and was directed to a few colleagues only.

The indiscretion lay not in the manner of distribution, but in putting the information in writing. Documentation increased the possibility that the information would fall into the wrong hands.

Protection

If people consistently end up getting the blame for things that go wrong, they will soon stop contributing. Solidarity among huddlers is necessary to protect participants from excessive blame or threats. Remember, one of the functions of the huddle is to undertake important work that cannot be accomplished by the formal organization. Sometimes the formal organization cannot afford to take the risks required to handle a situation. If confidentiality and loyalty are violated in the huddle, the risk to those involved rises, and the informal organization may also become vulnerable. Anyone who is a threat to others will not be included in the huddling process.

Mutuality

The question often arises as to whether participants in a huddle need to have the same temperament and working styles. The answer is definitely not. Huddles require compatibility, not uniformity. As a matter of fact, in most huddles complementary contributions—a diversity of interests, abilities, and talents—are needed to compensate for individual deficiencies and to get the work done. Those who come together in huddles must be able to communicate and share goals and interests. They can then join in the informal compact that allows them to do what needs to be done, with the assurance of cooperation and compatible viewpoints.

Much like a ball team, the informal organization needs a diversity of player talents and roles. This is part of what makes huddles so powerful.

Action

Effective working relationships require action, doing, carrying out understood roles and responsibilities. A person becomes a member of huddling relationships because others expect him to perform a certain role. Some individuals operate as idea generators; others work as implementors. Again, the unwritten rules of the organization and people's past contributions will subtly influence the roles they play.

Perhaps the most critical attribute of effective huddling is the ability to "fit in," to make the right contribution at a particular time so as to facilitate action and decisions. Those who detract from the work of others or ride as excess baggage will not be wanted. The ability to find a place, to work out an area of contribution and act as a positive influence on the accomplishments of others, is important to working effectively in huddles.

Controlled Self-Interest

The huddle is a goal-oriented, contributing entity in the organization. People who are perceived as pursuing *self-interest* to the detriment of the work of the group will not be valued or included in huddling processes. Such people will be cut out of the action and denied opportunities for leadership; their influence will be diminished significantly.

This does not mean that huddle participants cannot or do not pursue self-interests. What is critical is how the pursuit of self-interest is perceived. If it is seen as out of place, inordinately important to the individual, or detrimental to the work of the group, it will be interpreted as a violation of trust. The person will then be pushed aside or disciplined by the informal organization.

A businessman recently lost a very close, wealthy associate by recommending the quick sale of some of the associate's holdings, worth several million dollars. After the associate learned of the businessman's own speculative venture in another property, for which he needed considerable cash, he became suspicious of his friend's recommendation to sell. He subsequently cut off their business and personal relationships. Even if the businessman's motives had been pure, the appearance of self-interest was enough to destroy the trust he had built with his friend.

Outside Relations

A person may be effective in a given huddle but not trusted by other people in related huddles. As a result, the person's range of influence will be restricted. This can lead to problems if the person's strength is rooted in his ability to participate in a *network* of huddling relationships. A manager, for instance, may need to huddle near the top of the organization and at the same time retain close working relationships with peers and subordinates.

You need to be aware of potential conflicts among the huddles in which you participate. Just as it may be inadvisable to belong openly to the John Birch Society and the Communist party and expect to be accepted by both, so it may be difficult to participate in competing huddles. This example is, of course, extreme. But it does illustrate the importance of building trust and nurturing close relationships at multiple levels in the organization.

The important thing to keep in mind is that in order to exercise influence and provide leadership you must have productive working relationships with others. This is essential to your inclusion in various huddles and to your ability to make significant contributions to the organization.

12
Huddle
Decision Making

How are decisions really made in organizations? Formal processes for making more rational and "correct" decisions have received considerable attention in business and government circles. Management information systems, program planning, management by objectives, zero-base budgeting, value analysis, and other approaches are all efforts to improve rationality in decision making. But these are not the entire answer. Where other approaches fail, huddling surmounts troubles and gets results.

Organic Decisions

Huddling is best described as organic decision making. This contrasts markedly with the mechanical, formalized approaches that have received considerable attention in organizational literature. Huddle decisions arise out of troubles, needs, and natural relationships in organizational settings. Problems come up and are resolved by those willing and able to get involved. Issues are raised and opinions are expressed. Decision making in the informal organization is emergent, spontaneous, natural, and personal. It grows out of situations that demand action and, in many cases, is later sanctioned by the official organization.

It is hard to defend how some decisions are made. However, effective huddlers need to understand how they do occur. People rarely control matters as well as they wish, because they lack power and resources. Their knowledge of the future is limited, and they often have a shaky understanding of past and current situations. Thus many decision makers try to minimize risks; they are resistant to making drastic changes, taking big leaps forward.

Readiness for change seems to lag behind the need for change. It's hard to predict the results of certain actions. Unintended consequences inevitably undermine our efforts. Often it is difficult to get a responsible person to listen long enough to make a needed decision—if we can get to that person at all.

These conditions, and the natural checks and balances in any business or social situation, give huddling decision making its peculiar attributes. The process has been described as "muddling through." Organizational decisions normally are adjustments, not radical changes; incremental, not monumental; marginal, not fundamental; disjointed, not systematic and rational. Virtually all decision making is conservative and cautious. Seldom do we get all we seek. Usually we end up "giving in" a little even though we were really quite content with what we had. Sometimes our inability to change ourselves, others, or systems leads to a weakening of the organization through reduced profits or unsuccessful projects.

The Decision-Making Process

Effective huddling depends on the proper timing and sequencing of decision-making steps. First, those involved must recognize that something needs to be done. Then they must focus attention on the matter, discussing and analyzing it in detail while other demands compete for their time. Next, huddlers must search for the desired outcome, determining what is to be gained by making a decision or instituting a change. Huddlers can then identify the options available. Thereafter, they can gather data to determine what would happen if certain actions were taken. They must then evaluate those possibilities so they can make an intelligent choice and implement the decision, such as it turns out to be: pure or adulterated by compromise and tradeoffs.

Recess

People often suggest that a formal decision be delayed so they can think about it for a while. In this way, the formal process is recessed, adjourned so huddling can occur. If pushed too fast for a formal decision on an important issue, people will resist, delay, divert the matter so they can check things out with those affected and make needed adjustments.

Some people delay so that they can "posture" themselves properly, making sure their decision will be acceptable to clients, colleagues, voters, stock-holders, competitors, and anyone else who might react on a public or private basis. Other people call a recess in order to buy time, to make sure they are not being pushed too fast into something unwise.

One executive I know invariably resists any prop-osition made in a formal meeting. Some of his people have not learned how to handle this and still hit him head on time and again without success. Others have learned to introduce an idea as tentative, a proposal for him to think about. Later, in a more private and informal setting, they raise the idea again as some-thing they wish to implement, provided he does not object. Under those conditions he is usually positive, may give constructive suggestions, and normally ends up being supportive. The informal procedure gives him an opportunity to think the matter through, to avoid being pushed or rushed, and to keep a low pro-file of involvement until the idea is carefully evaluated and tested.

Shielding

Decision making in the official organization can be risky business. Within the confines of confidential huddling discussions, matters can be assessed realis-tically without concern for saving face or covering up.

If the formal organization takes an official position in haste or prematurely embarks on an action, vested interests can solidify too soon. If the official organiza-tion's course of action proves unacceptable for some reason, a "whitewash" or "smoothing over" is likely to occur to protect those involved. This is the essence of intraorganizational politics and one of the reasons that huddling is so pervasive in working environments.

Decision Premises

Huddlers need to understand the organization's decision-making premises—the unwritten procedures by which options are uncovered, data gathered, and evaluations made. Premises include the various taboos of the organization, definitions of right and wrong, priorities, fundamental organizational goals, and factors to be applied in all decision making.

If premises are not understood, the process of choosing and planning goes astray. Huddlers need to be realistic about what can and cannot be changed. They need to know what kind of obstacles will be encountered so they can devise some practical way to work around them.

Informal Contracts and Touching Base

Handshakes are the huddle's equivalent of a legal contract and are usually more binding than any written document.

Fortune magazine reported: "Nearly half of the hamburger patties McDonald's sells by the billions come from a company nobody ever heard of. In just eight years it's grown into a $200 million business. . . . Throughout this rapid growth McDonald's has remained Keystone's only customer. More interesting still, the company has been built, quite literally, on a handshake; Keystone has never had a contract with the folks at McDonald's headquarters in Oak Brook, Illinois." *

As decisions are "in process," huddlers need to know when they should consult again. That is, how far should they go before they touch base with each

* March 13, 1978.

other? These are matters that get worked out by informal understandings or by trial and error. Huddlers
should also know the difference between "touching
base" and "seeking permission" from someone else.
Sometimes people try to shift the risk to others by
asking their permission or pressing them for a
decision—instead of just touching base and proceed-
ing unless given a clear signal to halt. Hence,
huddlers must decide when to ignore, inform, coordi-
nate, consult, or get approval from someone else. All
these are important tactical considerations in the
decision-making process.

Decisiveness

Effective huddles need participants who are both
able and *willing* to accept responsibility. It is quite
natural to want to get rid of a "hot potato." In risky
situations, people will differ markedly in their willingness to get involved, to be decisive about what
should be done. Those who are indecisive and unwill-
ing to assume the risks of the informal organization are
inevitably pushed aside.

Co-workers of one senior officer I know will go to
almost any length to avoid taking a decision to him. If
they do confer with him, they withdraw at the first
sign of hesitation. If he wants to consider a matter,
they know they won't see it again for some time. As a
result, they often ignore problem situations and allow
them to deteriorate. Some huddlers, however, have
found ways to get the job done without him.

A troublesome counterpart to indecisiveness is the
usurpation of decision-making prerogatives that belong to someone else. People sometimes go too far in
making choices and taking action, overstepping the

bounds of their "authority." How far is too far? This is a matter of individual judgment; there are no hard-and-fast rules. But experience and careful observation should help you become "streetwise" in this matter. The key is to avoid being reluctant without becoming too eager. Recognize the need to check with others to be sure you have correct information, a proper perspective, and an on-target approach.

Hurdles

As decision-making deliberations occur, the nature of the obstacles should be understood. You need to know who can kill or table a particular course of action, who should be consulted on the matters involved and, ultimately, *who* decides. Timing is also critical. It is one thing to recognize the need to consult with certain people; it is quite another to recognize *when* certain individuals should be presented with recommendations so that a choice can be made. At some strategic point in the decision-making process—normally after much has occurred in informal huddles—the formal organization needs to be involved and an official decision made. This is how effective decision making takes place.

Conflict

Decision-making processes provide ample opportunities for conflict. Nonhuddlers react by fighting, blaming, and picking at each other. Or they take flight, abandoning the situation. Huddlers confront the issue directly, focusing on the problem itself rather than on blame or avoiding responsibility. A positive approach generally leads to the best results. Constructive problem solvers are most likely to be sought out for future problem-solving opportunities.

Decision making is clearly an important function of huddles. Huddles provide a degree of insulation for those who must make choices. They can bring together those people best qualified to participate. Huddling ensures the availability of the best information and the confidentiality required for effective decision making.

13
Communicating in Huddles

Top managers in one company made a confidential review of their field offices and concluded that several needed to be subdivided. Because their decision would affect a considerable number of people, they agreed to keep it guarded until an official announcement was made. After making their disclosure, the managers learned that everybody concerned already knew about it.

These managers failed to take into account the power of informal communication channels in the organization. Informal communication patterns are natural streams and tributaries, unlike the "engineered channels" found in the formal organization. Left alone, communication will flow in natural patterns through areas of least resistance. Like a stream of water winding through a mountain valley, communication moves from person to person and huddle to huddle wherever the message can get through.

Huddlers provide an array of data important to the organization: facts, observations, opinions, and tidbits. Before you contribute any of this information, you should know the personality of the people involved and their habits of behavior. People are interested in different kinds of information relevant to any given task. The data you provide should be tailored to the needs and working habits of your fellow huddlers.

A management analyst confided to me: "The report was fine, but I figured a few things were best left out. They were a little personal and would only make a stink rather than help. At the right time when I had a minute to mention them privately to Joe, he thanked me and asked what I would do. After I made a few suggestions, he began to use me in some new ways. We have been working rather closely ever since."

Packaging Messages

Effective communicators in the informal organization know what things are important in communication and how they should be "packaged" or transmitted as messages. There are several approaches to packaging information. You can focus on facts and figures, technical or expert opinions, or the judgments of experienced participants in the organization. You can handle communication as an emotional appeal or as an objective, straightforward process.

Circumstances will dictate the manner in which information is best presented. In some cases it is wise to first convey background information and facts. In other cases it is advisable to present conclusions first and then discuss how the conclusions were developed and what facts you have to support them.

One executive I know insists that his people bring him solutions, not problems. Another executive will fire anyone who presumes to do his thinking for him. He prefers to be told about the problem, after which *he* will think about it and discuss it with you. Then he will give *you* the solution. Huddlers who ignore the personalities of decision makers will have short-lived impact.

Shorthand

Efficiency is imperative in huddles. Communication within the huddle is normally cogent, with on-target, shorthand vocabulary developed to meet the needs of those involved. Huddling shorthand develops over time as people work together. Previous experiences make it possible to communicate without extensive explanations, definitions, or justifications. That is what shop talk is all about.

Those who must have things "spelled out" for them will not be included in huddling for long. If you don't know what "You take it from here" means, you're on the outs—and the meaning of that phrase differs from huddle to huddle. This is all part of understanding the "street language" of huddle culture.

Vocabulary

What is the appropriate vocabulary to use in transmitting information? Again, appropriateness depends on the individual or group involved. Certain language that would communicate effectively to some people may be misunderstood by others. People react differently to the connotations of words. Awareness of personalities should help you judge the likely effect of your communications as you transact huddling business.

Regardless of whom you're communicating with, be certain to avoid gobbledygook—official language that fails to get ideas through. A sample of what to avoid comes from a government agency report about cutting down on paperwork: "In order to accomplish this initial consolidation the EIA must conduct detailed functional and user requirements analyses, systems analyses, programmatic and respondent impact studies and cost/benefit analyses, as well as program, document, and implement all cancellations, modifications, and consolidations." *

Disclosures

Huddlers who have information need to decide what should be disclosed and whether disclosure should involve facts or opinions. In the interest of efficiency, you should avoid disclosing everything you know about a subject, unless you are in an extended huddle and full disclosure is called for. Huddlers must be sensitive to the types of information required by different individuals and should not disclose information when it would constitute a breach of confidentiality.

What is the proper timing of a disclosure? When should certain pieces of information be shared with others? In what sequence should matters be disclosed? With whom should information be shared— for whose "eyes or ears only"? How should confidentiality be handled? The answers to these questions

* *National Journal*, February 4, 1978.

usually call for judgment at the moment, but sometimes they can be determined beforehand as you exchange information and observations with others.

Protecting Sources

"Here it is, but if you quote me I'll deny it" is a protective statement often voiced by huddlers. In some cases, it is essential for huddlers to shield their sources of information. If information has come from other huddles in a network, from individuals who are not acceptable to others in the current group, or from someone who is a confidential informant to huddlers in other discussions, it may be highly inadvisable to disclose the *source* of the information. Trust is not to be breached.

Some journalists have refused to disclose the sources of information used in their news articles. Since much of the information comes from huddles, to violate this trust would destroy access to these sources. In a similar vein, the inside sharing of information among organizational workers sometimes requires a measure of confidentiality that in the huddler's judgment will need to be exercised.

Readiness

Because huddling processes are somewhat unpredictable—arising to meet issues or problems on demand—huddlers must be ready at any time with information that is relevant to current or potential problems. If a huddler repeatedly lacks relevant information, his value to other participants is diminished. On the other hand, if he seems to have information readily at hand, his stock will go up with other huddlers.

14
Huddling Roles

A PERSON is *included* in a huddle because of an ability to meet certain needs or to solve problems. Again, I emphasize the idea of inclusion rather than membership, which connotes a formal belonging or an official acceptance in a group. Inclusion suggests participation in an arena of relationships that are spontaneous and functional rather than formal or legal.

Primary and Secondary Huddlers

Participation in a huddle may be *primary* or *secondary*. Primary participants are an integral part of the huddle, involved in the substantive issues or problems being handled—contributors to the decision-making process. Primary participants exercise power and influence within the huddle and perhaps without. They initiate the huddle, determine the pace of activities, terminate phases of huddling activities, or terminate the huddle itself.

Secondary participants play a more peripheral role in huddles. They may act in a facilitative capacity, participating to gain or provide information. Or they may participate to further their own training and development, to help carry out some aspect of a decision, to serve as a witness to what happens, or to act as a "memory" for the group. Secondary participants often serve as connectors—links to other huddles in which they are involved. Both primary and secondary huddlers are necessary to provide a coherent stream of communications and decision making within a network of huddles.

Scope of Participation

The scope of a huddler's role is determined largely by his personality. Some huddlers are concerned about things close at hand—local matters, so to speak. Their concerns and activities do not range far beyond their jobs, the office in which they work, their company, or their hometown. Other huddlers are more cosmopolitan. They have a greater variety of interests and contacts, see farther into the future, move around geographically and socially, and are often less restricted by customs and formal roles.

Each type of huddler has a place in the informal organization. The "cosmopolitan" is often more of a strategist; the "local" is an implementor, a detail person who is going to be around to see things through.

Depth of Participation

Participation in huddles varies in degree. *Isolated* participation—involvement in only one or two huddling sessions—may occur because the person has a special contribution to make or because the problem is short-lived and can be quickly resolved. *Terminal* participation arises when a person fails to contribute meaningfully and is therefore not sought out for subsequent huddles. It may also occur if the situation suddenly changes and the huddling is no longer needed.

Intermittent participation arises out of a periodic need for information or contributions. People may participate intermittently because they have specialized ability or expertise, because they are unavailable on a regular basis, or because the huddle itself occurs on an intermittent basis. *Continuing* participation is closest to what might be termed "membership" in a huddle. Participants are involved on a regular basis and deal with a set of matters that have some continuity. In this case, compatible working styles and personalities are essential.

A continuing huddle may form around a group of executives whose formal positions call for interaction. They huddle on a regular basis before, during, or after meetings, at lunch, or on weekends to meet recurring situations. Continuing huddles may also develop among those who are not juxtaposed officially but who need to get together regularly to deal with matters left undone by the official organization. For instance, if an organization's reports are inadequate, a group of colleagues may huddle regularly to find out what's really happening or to identify and resolve problems that are overlooked in official reports.

Specialists and Generalists

Inclusion in huddling can be *specific* or *general*. People are included on a specific basis when their contributions are of a technical or specialized nature. Their utility in the huddle is limited, serving only the immediate needs of the group. In some cases, a specialist's role will broaden as he gains experience and is able to contribute more fully.

People are included on a general basis when they can serve a wide range of needs or perform several roles. Huddling generalists have the flexibility to make contributions in a number of areas. A classic example is Harry Hopkins, a long-time personal adviser to President Franklin Roosevelt.

Huddle Size and Term

Participation is affected by the size of the huddle. The role you play in a two-person huddle may differ significantly from your role in a huddle involving a number of individuals. If the huddle represents a small group—three to six individuals—some roles will be needed to facilitate the group's activity that are not required in a two-person huddle. The longer a huddle lasts, the greater the number and variety of roles that emerge. A short, fleeting work encounter between two people may appear to be the simplest of huddles, with limited roles, but often it requires greater skills and broader contributions than larger or more extended huddles.

Openers

Inclusion within a huddle does not come about because of academic degrees or formal credentials.

However, a college degree or a technical credential may prompt consideration of someone or, in rare cases, serve as a basis for testing a person to see if the credentials represent real capability. The same is true of past or present experience, formal positions, and status. All these are "door openers" but will not guarantee inclusion in a huddle on an intermittent or continuing basis.

Contacts within the formal or informal organization are other sources of entrée to huddles. They can also be highly functional in helping to connect the huddle to a larger, more powerful huddling network. Under these circumstances, contacts can be invaluable in carrying out huddling responsibilities.

A person's physical stature or image can often be a door opener. Some people "look like" they can, contribute meaningfully to huddles. This may gain them invitations and extended opportunities to prove themselves in a huddle, although they may eventually be dropped if they are not functional.

I once was asked to counsel a man prominent in the Kennedy administration. He was a "picture book" executive. The face, shoulders, hair, dress, demeanor, and stance were straight out of *Fortune* or *Business Week*. But once he got into a senior job, he was in trouble. His façade was penetrated repeatedly to reveal a lack of competence and technical expertise. He could throw up the right masks but couldn't put out results. Huddlers quickly found him out. My job was to promote insight and to suggest remedies, and we did make some progress. The point here is that, despite his image, this man was cut off from key huddling activities until he learned to contribute meaningfully.

The crucial test for inclusion in a huddle is whether a person can see what needs to be done and contribute productively in some way.

Role Playing

Huddles demand a variety of roles to be productive. As used here, the term "role" refers to the type of contribution made by a participant. The roles required in any given huddle depend on the nature of the activity undertaken, the maturity of the relationships among the participants, the number of people involved, and the length of time that the huddle will endure. Roles may also depend on whether the huddle is expected to extend into several sessions over time.

It is important to be perceptive about the types of roles that are productive in huddles. You should understand the various roles you play, analyze the roles played by others, identify new contributions that you or others could make, and call attention to any problems in "role casting" that may be undermining huddling activities. This kind of understanding and sense of responsibility can bring about vast improvements in the functioning of huddles.

Types of Roles

Initiator. The initiator kicks things off, prompts a huddling relationship, gets people together, introduces the problem or issue, and provides the start-up momentum for the huddle. Obviously, this role is extremely valuable and is often shared by two or more participants. Anyone who has a sense of responsibility and is looking for opportunities to contribute can serve as initiator.

Idea person. The idea person provides suggestions, proposes answers, and lays out options. The ideas may come from his own thought and analysis, from the experiences of others, or from observations of other situations.

Evaluator. The evaluator helps the group test ideas to make sure they are workable and in the best interests of everyone concerned. Typically, the evaluator asks penetrating questions or adopts an adversary role, suggesting that the huddlers not act until judgment has been exercised.

This function is epitomized by Clark Clifford, the Washington lawyer and former presidential adviser. President Lyndon Johnson called him "Just a Minute Clifford," with this explanation: "At the end of a discussion when we think we're all agreed, Clark would say, 'Now just a minute.' " * Clifford's role was to help put ideas in perspective, check on the thinking of the group, and look at things objectively and rationally.

Information gatherer. The information gatherer identifies the need for data or opinions, draws out available information from others, and suggests the need for additional information. At this point a participant may go to sources outside the huddle to obtain needed information. Or outsiders with information may be brought into the huddle.

Information can also be obtained from data banks, computers, manuals, reports, and files. The information gathering may take place while the huddle is still in session; or the huddle may be recessed and reconvened after information is available. The huddling network controls a great deal of this information sharing—who gets what, from whom, when, in what form, in what detail, and with what restrictions.

*Jack Anderson, *The Washington Post,* February 26, 1977.

Strategist. The strategist formulates an approach to resolving the issue at hand. The approach may focus on how the group will work together to take care of the problem or on how the issue will be handled by the formal organization. In the one case, the strategy focuses on the operations of the huddle itself; in the other, it focuses on the solution that will be implemented as a result of actions within the huddle. Both are needed to promote cooperation among huddlers and to expedite the handling of the problem. Strategists must be able to think in abstract terms, but they must also be realistic about what can be done.

Tension reliever. The tension reliever's role is often valuable to a huddle. A tense situation can be eased by telling a joke, suggesting that the group break, interjecting an appropriate (or even inappropriate) story, or citing an analogous situation. The tension reliever may even change the subject so that huddlers can reflect on the matter and come back to it later when the issue can be handled constructively. If carried too far, this role can become a distraction, destroying the focus of the huddle. Such a disruption must be handled sensitively by other participants.

Process guide. Most people focus on the problem at hand without giving adequate attention to *how* it should be approached. The process guide asks the questions: "Where do we start on it?" "What's the next step?" "Is this the best approach?" "What about first looking at options and then getting into data?"

Fixer. The fixer is the troubleshooter, identifying what's holding things up, what went wrong, how to get everything to hang together until the job is finished. The fixer is sometimes a tinkerer, fussing with things to get them to go more smoothly. If carried to an extreme, however, he becomes a cobbler—a nonhud-

dler who does more harm than good by emphasizing
structure and efficiency at the expense of accomplishment.

Disciplinarian. The disciplinarian keeps matters
on track and weeds out extraneous topics. Often he
acts as a watchdog on inappropriate behavior ("Harry,
you'll trip us all up if you go at it that way"), suggests
trimming off unproductive associates ("Leave him out
of it"), helps maintain proper pacing ("Come on, you
guys!" "Where's that report you promised me today?"), and keeps things legal ("Hey, it's against the
law!" "The policy is explicit on this and we've got to
be tough").

Decision getter. The decision getter calls for action, suggests the need for a decision, buttons things
down. This sometimes requires breaking a logjam,
clarifying the issue to be decided, or focusing people's
attention on the decision at hand rather than on side
issues. The decision getter calls for a vote: "Okay,
now, what's our decision, A or B?"

Decision maker. The decision maker says "Let's
do this" or "Here is what we will do." Like the decision getter, his role is critical. Otherwise huddlers
would be left in an indecisive state, confused and frustrated. The ability to suggest that the time has come
for a decision (the role of the decision getter) contrib-
utes to the "pacing" of the group. The ability to affirm
a decision allows the group to culminate its activities.

Implementor. Once a decision has been made, the
implementor makes sure that appropriate action is
taken. His role involves apportioning responsibilities
and duties among those who will follow through. The
implementor pulls things together so that something
happens. This may require highlighting a matter that

has been dropped and seeing that it is given proper attention. Or it may involve devising a follow-up plan.

Closer. The closer suggests that the work has been done and that the huddlers can move on to other things. This can be done through a timely question ("Is that it, then? Can we move on it?") or a flat closing statement ("Let's wrap it up"). Or the closer may simply express thanks to participants. All these techniques close out the huddle satisfactorily.

Termination

Under certain conditions it may be necessary to terminate a huddle or to restructure huddling relationships. This problem arose in one corporation that sought my counsel. The president and a number of key executives were old-timers who had grown up with the company. They comprised an informal "club" and had access to each other. But over the years the company grew too big for this arrangement. Too many people were coming to the president for decisions and advice. He was being pulled into matters that should have been handled elsewhere. Those managers who were not part of the "club" resented their exclusion and the advantages enjoyed by those on the inside.

Fortunately, the president recognized what was happening. I was called in to coach him and his immediate staff. We explored options and put together a strategy for fostering new huddling relationships that were in keeping with current times and that would protect the president from excessive demands from associates.

People cease participating in a huddling relationship for several reasons. Sometimes a conflict arises with participation in other huddles. For instance, when confidentiality is threatened because of continued inclusion in other groups, it may be necessary to drop out of a huddle.

Often people simply outgrow the relationships represented in a huddle: a relationship that was once useful and functional is no longer productive. For example, promotion in the formal organization may make it inappropriate to continue some huddling relationships. In other cases, people simply overextend themselves. Their huddling relationships create excessive demands and a cutback is necessary.

Termination of a huddling relationship may also come by directive: an influential official "orders" you to stay away from certain individuals or to cease participating in certain activities. In this case, your association with various people may be creating a bad impression, or you may be running too high a risk that the activities represented in a huddle will undermine your position in the organization.

Active participation in a huddle may be superseded by greater opportunities in more influential huddles, contact with more influential people, or involvement with more significant problems and issues. Even so, it is usually wise to maintain "contacts" in several spheres of the organization, not only to keep in touch with what's happening but also to extend your influence in the huddling network.

Strategies for Withdrawal

Avoidance. One way to terminate involvement in a huddle is sheer avoidance. You can stop interacting with certain individuals, not meet with them, or deliberately avoid "running into them." Or you can explain that you no longer have the time to deal with issues of concern to the huddle. You can indicate that your needs are being met through other means and that further involvement would therefore be a waste of time. In terminating in this manner, you should avoid suggesting that you are now "better than" your one-time huddling associates; it seldom makes sense to alienate others.

Diminished contribution. Another strategy for terminating a huddling relationship is to diminish your input to the group, to cease offering information or suggestions. In effect, you become a noncontributor. You can suggest your diminished interest through nonverbal means or through halfhearted or lighthanded responses to matters at hand.

As a supervisor, for example, you may have engaged in a number of huddles to help a subordinate grow in his assignments. If that relationship becomes excessively burdensome and unproductive, you probably should withdraw. You can do so by showing less enthusiasm for the relationship or by indicating that you are going to have to cut back on your time and that the subordinate will have to stand on his own.

Going formal. You can also withdraw from huddling relationships by "going formal." If people are trying to continue a huddle, you can suggest that they see someone else, ask them to check with your secretary for an appointment, or indicate that you can't talk about the matter at the moment and put them off either temporarily or indefinitely. Recognize the cost of these actions, however. You may alienate co-workers, lose goodwill, and shut off future trust and working relations.

Try transferring a matter previously handled in huddling relationships to a meeting. That is, move the matter to the formal organization, where it will likely be killed, lost, or slid out into another huddle. When pressed in a huddle to deal with the matter, you can argue that it will be brought up in the meeting or should be handled by the formal organization. In this approach you formalize the relationship by refusing to consider the matter in huddles.

Finding a surrogate. Another way to diminish involvement in a huddle is to find a surrogate to play your role. You can suggest that someone else supply the information or carry out the tasks that you have previously handled. If possible, you should suggest a specific person for this job.

In effect, you are delegating communication and decision-making responsibilities to a deputy. Your representative does not necessarily have to be a subordinate in the formal organization. He may be your peer or even someone superior to you in the formal organization—your boss or a senior staff person. Whatever the case, your surrogate should be in an active huddling relationship with you elsewhere. You can then keep in touch and benefit from the huddling that is going on without placing excessive demands on your time.

IV
Huddling
Improvements

*H*UDDLING can always be improved. How can the official dimensions of the organization help? This section presents several ideas for improving your performance in huddles and the performance of others.

15
Bridling Huddles

T HE formal organization isn't helpless. It can exercise some influence over huddling activities. We know that many organizations are out of control. But huddling doesn't need to be so unchecked. As an organization worker and executive coach, I've found a number of huddle-bridling approaches that work quite well. If you are a frustrated formal organizational worker, some of these approaches—or adaptations of them—may help.

Performance and Accountability

One way to keep huddles under control is for a manager to officially set explicit goals with organizational units. Establish and document specific achievements or deadlines, and let people know the quality of results you expect. Work from real priorities, not wish lists. Get a clear understanding about when you will check up, then do it. Establish any groundrules needed, but don't invent extras. Be tough on results and evaluate performance. Teams of workers generally respond to a reasonable challenge when they feel supported and recognized.

Communicate clearly what you want from each subordinate. Focus on the *results* you expect, not just smokescreen motions and activities. Get together privately with subordinates and review their accomplishments periodically. Be sure you are on target with real organizational priorities. Avoid sending out foggy signals—stop-and-go orders that muddle things in between your accountability interviews. If workers know they will have to make an accounting on a regular basis, they will pay more attention to getting results.

Be very clear about what is out of bounds. Standards need to be clearly established and reviewed. No ambiguity should exist about what is permissible. Illegal acts are out. People count. No violence. Serve the customer. Consider the public interest. Profits are to be pushed. Et cetera.

Emphasize the unique *values* of the organization. These are not manufactured; they grow up out of organizational culture and precedents. They define boundaries as well as core concerns and priorities. Make certain that values are known and accepted, not as niceties but as imperatives. When huddlers know you mean business, you will have one good rein on what happens in the informal organization.

Assessing Candidates

Both huddlers and nonhuddlers often use the "buddy system" to get people promoted in the organization. This sometimes has a seamy as well as practical side, so be cautious. Formal organizations have a spotty record for getting the right people into key jobs. Informal processes can also produce incompetents—cronies, loyalists, and trusted assistants who are not cut out for promotion.

Several techniques can be used to overcome weaknesses of both the informal and formal organization in this tug-of-war over promotions. Begin by defining the requirements for success in your key jobs. Make these criteria clear and understandable to workers. Advertise them. This will help workers see the need to develop in order to compete successfully. They can then "screen themselves" to determine if they are truly cut out for the work. Encourage nominations from throughout the organization.

One important caveat: make sure you use an independent, objective process to screen nominees. The criteria applied in screening should include leadership dimensions. Frequently, those closest to home are best able to judge the technical competence of workers. You should retain in the net only those who can clearly do the job. These successful nominees comprise a "pool of candidates" from which choices are to be made by selecting officers. In theory, anyone in the pool can do the particular job or jobs involved.

It is very important that your screening technique have *face validity*. That is, it must be straightforward and believable to workers, managers, and selecting

officers. It cannot be mysterious, complicated, or
obscured by professional jargon, statistics, conjec-
tures, and abstractions. Personal interviews, psychological tests, and similar techniques are useful, but
they do not meet all the requirements for validity.

Rules

Make rules that will get at the problems you perceive. Cut out rules that no longer apply, that don't
win you anything anyway. Don't make policies has-
tily. Consider informal, low-profile approaches
whenever possible. Make certain you have the support of those who can make or break you in enforcing
your intended rules.

Keep rules simple. People won't apply what they
cannot understand. Help those involved understand
why. Explain what you are doing. Avoid bureaucratic
jargon and overly legal language. If you must satisfy
the lawyers, provide others with a lay translation of
what you are saying. Introduce new policies or rules
as if you are dealing with human beings—because you
are. Put things in writing (in most cases), but avoid
acting as if the target for change is an "office" when
you know very well it's live, feeling, thinking, habit-
prone people. They are the ones who have to "consider" your rule and decide whether to be cooperative. Your concern, therefore, is to make each rule "effective." This will require (1) devising the right rule
for a particular circumstance and (2) introducing it in
an acceptable manner.

Discipline and Control

Don't be afraid to discipline. Step into an unproductive huddle and take action. You can't seal off and

stop huddling. But you can call a halt to things that shouldn't be going on. The Nixon White House might have survived if someone had stepped in to give the "stop order."

Warn nonhuddlers, ineffective huddlers, off-track huddlers. Intervene to establish new directions, inject more valid information, curb outrageous rumors, or otherwise cut off something you consider unwise. People can be fired, demoted, transferred, pulled off an assignment, or reprimanded. If a situation appears troublesome, weigh the potential gains and risks and do what you feel is right. Don't ignore contracts (with unions or individuals), laws, administrative procedures, taboos, or other restrictions and imperatives. Most of all, never think you can do nothing. Incompetency is always a ground for disciplinary action, including dismissal.

Send new faces into the ring, onto the field. If matters call for your influence, inject yourself in huddling relationships. Thrust in your own personality, experience, authority, convictions, persuasiveness. Flex your muscles. Raise your voice and be heard. Let people know you are around. Be assertive. Get your allies lined up. By sending in new players, you can upset any new power balances that are forming. Your surrogates can speak for you and, certainly, listen for you. Get involved when you must—to accelerate the tempo of activities, to thwart usurpation of your legitimate authority, and to ensure consideration of your point of view.

If things become too loose—laissez-faire, anything goes—assert formal authority more visibly, discipline more swiftly and clearly. If the atmosphere is too uptight, foster camaraderie and friendly interpersonal relations. Promote a more democratic climate by sharing problem-solving roles and opening up huddling activities. In any organization, key individuals can set the mood and climate for others. In fact, the organization's climate is a collective expression of the attitudes and personalities of the folks involved.

Consultant Checks

I was once asked to work with the president of a large banking system that was experiencing astonishingly rising loan losses. I observed the officers and made a careful diagnosis of the behavior of each contributing decision maker. The problem soon became clear. A key second-level executive, underneath his tough façade, was extremely vulnerable to political pressure. It was hard for him to make any technical decision that was subject to review by higher officials.

Because of his insecurity, this executive had been "massaging" the data and recommendations on large loan applications that he submitted to the bank's executive committee. He recognized that the committee often considered "political matters" along with technical factors in its decisions. Not wanting to lose face, he began entering into informal, huddling-type activities to determine how best to slant his recommendations to his superiors.

The members of the executive committee were not aware of the soft, politically tempered recommendations they were getting. In their own huddling sessions they would factor in considerations that the executive had already allowed for. Out of this came weak loans and disturbing losses. Their business had prospered with the one-stage huddling, but when the executive's "prehuddling" became a pattern, business took a sharp downward turn.

Fortunately, the company recognized the need for huddle harnessing and decided to take action. I was called in to counsel with those involved. The ground-rules for reviewing loan applications were reaffirmed and personnel changes were made. Eventually, loan losses returned to an acceptable level.

An outside, third-party "eye and ear" can be a valuable check on how things are going in your organization. In large companies internal consultants may do the job, but often outsiders will be more credible and objective. Consultants can discover the extent of huddling, the types of matters being handled, weaknesses in the formal organization that are spawning huddles, and damages inflicted by nonhuddlers. Consultants can suggest ways that improvements can be made.

Organizational structure needs to be checked out regularly, and it should be as functional as possible. The answer is not always harnessing huddles. In many cases, official aspects of the organization need to be aligned more closely with a productive, healthy informal organization.

Aggressors

Ambitious, impatient youngsters with high potential often become troublesome to the organization. Without discipline and proper challenges, they can create havoc. Don't team them with mumblers, hobblers, or coddlers. They will run amok under those conditions. Instead, pair them with experienced huddler coaches.

My father used to team up a promising, rambunctious young horse with a composed, seasoned animal. They would learn to pull together. The "charger" would become productive more quickly under these circumstances. People are not that different. You don't develop a charged-up new employee with a straightjacket or with excessive freedom. Proper assignments, strategically timed, with a coaching companion will bring results.

16
Huddling Agenda

W<small>HAT</small> do huddlers talk about? Almost everything. What *should* be their concern? Issues that will help organizations work better. Huddlers need an agenda that helps them make a distinction.

So far, we have focused almost entirely on the *process* of huddling—why and how it occurs. But, we also need to pay attention to the *content* of huddles—the substantive issues and problems that the informal organization needs to resolve. The official organization is no better at ferreting out essential issues than it is at dealing with them once they are identified. Organizations spend most of their energies fighting isolated troubles—often symptoms, not the real problems. Huddlers need to do better—and they generally do.

I have learned that the success of any organization

is determined by a few essential matters. At some point the agenda of huddlers needs to cover these matters. Otherwise, the organization is going to suffer. Huddlers should be alert to the imperatives for an effective organization. Here are the matters that count.

Entrepreneurial Leadership

Somebody somewhere needs to point the direction. People need a common purpose and approach if they are to work together. Usually objectives are set when organizations are born. Often, they are lost along the way. Every *successful* organization knows where it is going—what it is trying to accomplish.

This may seem painfully elementary. You're right. It is. It is so basic that most workers miss it altogether.

I once consulted with a senior executive of a *Fortune* 500 company. I asked him to describe the mission of his division. He hesitated, pondered, then deferred the question until later. His inability to respond clearly and promptly was the root of a problem that was manifesting itself throughout the division. Workers were not sure what they were supposed to be doing, how they fit in, or how they should be spending their time. But my question to the executive set off a chain reaction of positive changes that led, ultimately, to increased productivity throughout the division.

One of the first items on a huddler's agenda is to provide vision and perspective—the hallmarks of entrepreneurial leadership. New opportunities for the organization need to be identified and integrated with the old. People must be motivated to pursue those opportunities. Somewhere the products, services, and programs need to be formulated, then reexamined and updated. The establishment of objectives is the key. Those who set them have already exercised power.

Organizational strategy is critical. How will the organization's activities be coordinated? Will this be a centralized or a decentralized operation? Will success be pursued through superior products that "sell themselves" or through a strong salesforce that pushes midrange products? Myriad variations on these questions could be asked, but the central question is: How will the business of the organization be carried out? Somebody decided that matter at the beginning— deliberately or inadvertently. The issue needs to be reexamined repeatedly by conscientious huddlers.

The essence of the entrepreneur's role is to identify an opportunity and to build something to take advantage of it. This is true for a fledgling, shoestring operation or for an established, successful giant. It applies equally to industrial, government, and other institutions. Organizations as well as people must adapt to new situations and stay on top of new trends in order to survive.

Resource Management

People never seem to have enough of what they really want. Resources are always limited: only so much money can be borrowed, taxed, or drawn from savings. Eventually everything runs out—time, goodwill, energy, you. To think otherwise is to court disaster. The resources that are essential to a business must not only be guarded but deployed to gain maximum return. Resources are essential to achievement of any kind.

Scarcity calls for business planning, efficient work

methods, and intelligent application of technologies, equipment, and facilities. Raw materials—ore, grain, data, ideas—must be identified and secured. In each case, practical know-how, properly applied and executed, is critical.

Advanced techniques for directing and managing resources so as to achieve objectives have been tried throughout organizational history. These include management systems, goal setting, financial planning, work design, industrial engineering, and project and program management. Huddlers should be ready to contribute in these areas.

Resource Exchange

To survive, organizations and people must exchange something they possess for something they want. Services, products, technology, and know-how are bartered. This exchange then provides resources to further pursue objectives. Organizations acquire resources through marketing, advertising, selling, taxing, borrowing, assessing, billing, investing, lending, issuing bonds, selling stock, contracting, soliciting, and building public support.

Thus resource exchange is another key item on the huddler's agenda. Huddlers must be aware of the ever pertinent question: What do we have that someone else wants or that we can induce someone to buy? Through the proper exchange of resources new life is given to the enterprise.

People Recruitment

Organizations don't work without people. They never have. They never will. Someone must get people into organizations so they can contribute whatever is needed from them, whether it be their muscle power, technical expertise, creativity, leadership, or entrepreneurial ability.

Recruiting people for whatever purpose involves several challenging tasks: establishing personnel needs, setting hiring standards, announcing vacancies, finding candidates, assessing the capability and potential of applicants, and devising salary and incentive systems. Huddlers get involved in all these tasks because they know recruitment is essential to the well-being of the organization.

Socialization

Organizations come in all sizes: from a dozen employees to hundreds of thousands. It is a challenge to the organization to help people who are working together—whatever their numbers—feel a sense of belonging and a desire to contribute and cooperate.

Both the formal and informal organizations should play a part in building solidarity among employees, instructing them in the organization's purpose and structure, and explaining how decisions are made and carried out.

Getting people into the operation is handled formally through orientation and training programs, manuals, memoranda, bulletins, meetings, and various career development programs. But informal processes can often be more powerful. For example, a respected employee tells a new worker, "That's not the way we do things around here." This simple statement can have a powerful effect on the newcomer and, if repeated in various forms and under various circumstances, on workers throughout the organization. This shaping of attitudes and actions is the heart of the informal socialization process.

Contributions

Employees ought to produce something constructive. They don't always do so. Some employees don't contribute at all. If people don't work on the organization's purpose, the organization won't work either. Various techniques have been tried to encourage people to contribute: defining missions and goals, parceling out duties among workers, establishing superior–subordinate relationships, and writing job descriptions, performance contracts, and standards of performance. Wage and salary systems, incentive packages, awards and recognition, and skill development are other techniques for trying to get people to accept responsibility and do something constructive. Human relations techniques, job enrichment, and team building have also been used.

These formal approaches are usually clear and well known to huddlers. The approaches available to the informal organization are often obscure: the pat on the back, a new, challenging assignment, a sign of approval from a superior. That is what much of this book is about. Huddlers need to participate actively in this dimension of organizational work—even if the outcome is a more formalized structure for getting people to contribute.

Order

Left to themselves, most organizations would drift. Something must be done to shape activities into a consistent pattern. Both the formal and informal organization can help to control disruption and to strike the proper balance between stability and change.

Formal procedures used to accomplish this include: rules, regulations, policies, disciplinary actions, information and management systems, delegations of legal authority, manuals, legislation, administrative procedures, performance evaluations, and reports. Huddling offers some other alternatives— among them, affirmative control (Chapter 9) and huddle bridling (Chapter 15). The point is that huddlers too should feel responsible for creating stability and order in the organization.

Adaptation

Organizations work better when they are in tune with reality. Opportunities change. Fads and technologies come and go. Public opinions shift. Competition grows and ebbs. These conditions must be monitored and adjusted when necessary to keep the organization functioning.

Formal attempts to do this include performance tracking and analysis, policy and program reviews, product evaluation, issue analysis, problem solving, environment monitoring, and research and development. Forecasting, value analysis, technology review, market research, and consultant studies have also been tried.

Changes in policies, organizational structure, regulations, personnel practices, and work procedures help the formal organization adjust to meet the demands and opportunities of the future. Changes in attitudes, values, relationships, and other aspects of the informal organization are harder to make. Formal efforts to direct these social conditions usually fail, because attitudes, feelings, values, and personalities cannot be legislated. Training programs often fall short in their results.

Huddlers must recognize that change is needed if organizations are to work well. The informal organization can be very powerful in making needed adaptations through behind-the-scenes negotiations and laying the groundwork for formalized meetings. The official organization needs to be made congruent with the informal organization in order to get significant work accomplished. This ought to be on the agenda of responsible huddlers.

17
Huddle Leadership

T HE head of a large research organization once asked me to assess the leadership potential of several candidates for a division director's position. He sent me six final candidates and (out of curiosity) a seventh, a noncandidate who lacked the professional credentials normally required. My partner and I engaged the candidates in a series of collective and individual work assignments. We observed their attitudes and skills for two days, assessing their development and potential for the job. We then submitted our analyses to management.

After reviewing our findings, top executives in the organization gave the noncandidate the job. In the unstructured work assignments he had recognized the roots of leadership. Even though he was an outsider, he quickly won the respect of his competitors. He structured their work, provided direction, resolved troubles, used the power sources available, and contributed significantly to accomplishing the work of the group. In his new position with the research organization, he has shown the same qualities.

There is a difference between being "in charge" and being "a leader." Huddles need leaders—acutely so, since huddling must compensate for leadership gaps in the formal organization.

Leadership can take two forms: structural and interpersonal. Structural leadership is accomplished through implementing new policies, infusing new ideas, changing formal relationships, altering physical environments, and adjusting forms, reports, and information flows. Interpersonal leadership is face to face, usually one on one. It involves people directly. Structural leadership affects people only secondarily and may well get worked out through interpersonal means. Structural leadership often is the second stage of the overall leadership process.

How is leadership exercised in huddles? Huddle leadership is interpersonal—a process of recognizing opportunities and then achieving results with others. There are eight major roots that nourish this type of leadership.

Power

To influence events and people, a leader must have power. The sources of power include professional and technical expertise, formal positions, legal rights, knowledge of policies and procedures, and control of resources and services.

Power depends on interpersonal skills—the ability to persuade, motivate, and organize. Access to influential people in the organization enhances power, as does access to vital information. The capacity to dominate and intimidate others when necessary and the ability to resist domination are also important.

The capacity to lead is one thing; the courage to act decisively to make strategic use of power reserves is what finally counts. These power sources, used together, can be a tremendous benefit in getting results. They allow leaders to move the organization in a meaningful direction toward the achievement of key objectives.

Prominence

A leader is visible, known by others. Prominence is essential to being heard and getting results. Only rarely is visibility inadvisable for a leader.

Several things can build a huddler's prominence: having high status with associates, having his name and face recognized, being in good standing with higher-ups in the organization, and having visible skills and expertise. Awards, honors, titles, status symbols, and formal education also build prominence. People pay attention to someone they know is marked for leadership, someone who is seen as a "comer." It helps to be seen as a winner in some other setting, but not to the neglect of job responsibilities.

No one of these factors will guarantee you a leadership role, but they will surely accrue to your *potential* for leadership.

Respect

Leadership is built not only on prominence but on respect—on gaining a *favorable* reputation with others. Respect comes, in part, from success in past work assignments, popularity, commitment, loyalty, trustworthiness, ethical standards, and strong convictions. If you show a concern for the rights and well-being of others and a tolerance for individual differences, you usually win respect from others. Dependability, conscientiousness, consistency, integrity, self-control, self-confidence are also positive factors in the ability to exercise leadership.

Sensitivity

Leaders must be sensitive to what is going on around them, especially to those matters relevant to their work. They must be receptive to feedback—even disagreeable news or hard-to-swallow criticism—and be attuned to informal sources of information and the opinions of others. If you are serious about providing leadership in huddling activities, you must be awake, alert, and ready to respond. Focus on your intellectual development and make sure you are free from prejudice and distortions. Do all you can to be up to date on events, to have timely information, and to maintain good listening habits.

Direction

Leaders need to have ideas about directions and destinations. Developing specific goals and objectives, working out a practical course of action, taking initiative, getting things moving, and keeping matters on track all contribute to leadership. Persuasiveness, constructive aggression, forward thinking, and a "can do" attitude provide direction for others.

Structuring

Plans are not self-executing. Order does not impose itself on people. Most things disintegrate or remain in various stages of disarray when left alone. Effective leaders see that activities get structured and help others work together more smoothly and productively.

In organizing work activities, you must let others know what is expected of them. Define roles, responsibilities, and results to be achieved. Build teamwork, pull loose ends together, support your co-workers, strengthen feelings of belonging, and schedule activities.

A few businesses are structuring work around "autonomous work teams"—small groups that are assigned complete units of work (assembling a complete product, for instance). Workers in each group establish their procedures, roles, responsibilities, and in some cases their work hours. In certain respects these groups can be viewed as large, continuous huddles. They get performance feedback directly from the work itself and handle their own quality control, supervision, scheduling, and discipline. There are many variations on this technique, but all are built on notions about people and work that are consistent with huddling processes.

As a leadership-oriented huddler, you should curtail disruption by others and help to formulate needed policies, procedures, and practices in the organization. Set a good example through your own work habits and personal organization. If you are confused and in disarray, you will have a difficult time establishing order and maintaining discipline among those you work with.

Handling Conflict

Troubles don't go away. They just put on a new face and reappear. If something irksome or dysfunctional can happen, it probably will. Leaders should be prepared for conflict, not surprised or disheartened by it. Count on people not getting along perfectly. Short-fused crises come up and must be handled. Someone needs to face direct and open showdowns, to help resolve conflicting demands by others. Leaders must be poised and confident under stress while facing diverse people and shifting situations in the organizational ruckus.

Achievement

A good record for producing results is essential to leadership. People like to be teamed with a winner, a doer. A losing team seldom enjoys the satisfaction of a successful one. Personal drive and effort can add to the luster of achievement. People seldom follow a laggard. Persistence and endurance count, as do health, and vitality.

Remember that to be a leader you must know your strengths. Take advantage of whatever power you have. Spend it wisely. Work on building your visibility and reputation to suit your situation. Provide direction and order. Be sensitive to what's going on around you. Take some risks to get involved. Be a doer—an achiever—and work selflessly for the success of others.

18
Coaching Huddlers

Not all workers are natural-born huddlers. But huddlers can be developed and improved. The fact that huddling is a natural response to difficult organizational conditions doesn't mean it should be left entirely in its natural state. Most workers are formally educated in technical and specialized matters, not leadership or huddling. Few are prepared for the human aspects of organizational work. Employee training seldom meets many crucial needs of workers. Most organizations get little "change" from their training dollar.

The development of most workers occurs as a natural, ongoing process. People grow on the job as they are challenged, gain new insights, and experience different working environments. They pick up ideas from co-workers and develop some of their own. Any organized training by the formal organization competes with this natural learning and growth.

Coaching

When huddlers are developed well, the process usually involves a "coach" who shows, tells, suggests, warns, disciplines, and rewards. A coach may be a helpful boss, respected peer, friend, or associate. Huddlers may have several coaches and receive suggestions from various people.

Coaches face the challenge of communicating matters that are not always discreetly talked about in public, particularly when doing so throws the spotlight on sensitive events within the organization. Privacy and trust—psychological safety—are needed so that these frank discussions can happen, with candid questions and straightforward counsel.

Coaching usually occurs in one-on-one development huddles. Coaches teach procedures and principles: time-worn, tried-and-tested ideas that work, concepts that are relevant and timely. This counsel is given *when* the huddler is most prepared to receive it. A huddler's readiness to learn is often created by troubles, challenges, or new opportunities.

One of my clients recently received the Distinguished Achievement Award for Management from a member of the President's Cabinet. It was the only award for "management" given to anyone in the department that year. Three years earlier, this man had been in serious trouble. Staff turnover was very high, relations with the employee association were literally at the "shoving" stage, and suspicion and mistrust were deep. His personal image was in disrepair. His turnabout since that time has been steady and consistent. The improvements have not come about by attending management courses. He doesn't read management books or articles. He espouses no coherent theory of management. Instead, over the past three years he and I have huddled frequently.

Since I made my strategic intervention (initiated by the department's senior management and labor group), this "honored" manager and I have had consistent and far-ranging coaching sessions, generally unscheduled and unstructured. We have explored the roots of his successes and difficulties, needed changes, the timing of his actions, his progress, and areas for fine-tuning. Once our relationship was established and he wanted to improve, the coaching began quietly, inconspicuously, line upon line—and it continues yet.

Insights

A good coach is a teacher, a special kind of teacher. He not only conveys ideas but also observes and then demonstrates the connection between the ideas and the huddler's actual behavior. Coaches provide feedback, giving huddlers the insights they need to make improvements.

A coach needs to encourage people to change. The status quo can be disastrously comfortable. Personal change disrupts habits, relationships, and biases. Huddlers first must see a need—a personal need—for a change. They must then be shown *how* to change. After changing, huddlers need encouragement, incentives, and other inducements to maintain their new path.

Modeling

Coaches teach huddlers to feel responsible for making changes. In this effort, *the qualities of the coach are the model.* If the coach is viewed as successful and credible, as a willing and authentic source of help, the coach's model serves as an important base for accountability.

The coach does not have to be perfect. The huddler is not molded in the image of the coach: individual differences and the fallibility of coaching make this impossible. Coaching requires, not emulation but credibility on the part of the coach and a desire to improve on the part of the huddler.

Scouting

Not everyone is suited to the disorderly huddling process. Many people are frustrated by the ambiguity and conflict of huddles. Others reject huddling outright as overly political and devious. They see the underside rather than the responsible and productive side. Frequently they are turned off by hasslers, hustlers, and other nonhuddlers. Some of these people can never profit from serious coaching effort. Others can be reclaimed.

Coaches should be on the lookout for those with huddling talent and draw them into more productive activity. They should watch for people who can tolerate ambiguity, accept the risk of working in the informal organization and the realities of huddling activity, think strategically, and deal with the competition of the informal organization.

Shaping

Huddlers do not develop overnight; they need time to grow. Emerging huddlers are willing to venture out, get involved, experiment with new skills, see things better, shape up, try again. During this learning process, *experiences* themselves begin to instruct the huddler.

Huddlers must learn from their own experience—nature's feedback—or else they will slip into muddling, mumbling, or fumbling. Coaches can help immensely by warning, instructing, correcting, suggesting "how to," and expressing approval or disapproval. Some of these techniques are, of course, nonverbal; others are explicit and overt.

Through experience and coaching, huddlers can pick up the vital insights they need to operate in the foray: information about the personalities of fellow workers, working relationships into which they must fit, the sources of real power, booby traps, and likely pitfalls.

Huddlers often benefit from a coach's candid opinion about management systems and decisions, organizational breakdowns, out-of-date policies and practices, and real priorities.

Through developmental huddles employees get information about how they are "really doing"—whether they are making it in their work and careers. Coaches can tell people where they stand. This feedback and counsel help immeasurably in giving coaches the opportunity to shape the behavior and outlook of huddlers.

Assessing Leadership

While consulting with a well-known corporate giant, I met a division director who told me how he got to be a manager. He was the best technician around, had written acclaimed papers, and represented the company at national and international professional meetings. He was working on pioneering research that might lead to a Nobel prize. He was caught off guard when offered a management assignment, then dismayed when pressed to accept. To escape, he took a year's leave of absence, left the country, and returned expecting the management job to have been filled. He was greeted with another request to accept the management responsibilities. When he declined, he was threatened with: "Okay, Tom will be your new boss." He accepted rather than work under Tom. But within a year he left the company to get away from the mass of people problems and administrative paperwork under which he felt buried.

Many natural-born followers, like this executive, fall or are shoved into leadership assignments. Outstanding technical performers are often "rewarded" with promotions into management ranks. In most organizations I have worked with, between 30 to 50 percent of those nominated for supervisory assignments lack essential skills for working with others. This leadership cadre needs to be strengthened significantly in almost all organizations.

Coaches can play a significant role in assessing leadership potential and developing leadership skills. Leaders are both born *and* made. Nonleaders can be coached to develop the skills they need to manage others. Those with natural gifts for leading can be identified early. They are found every day. Without help they emerge, rise up, just happen. Many potential leaders are now missed and misused. Countless come to the fore tardy. Some get discouraged and sidetracked by harsh realities before they gain confidence and self-esteem required to sustain leadership.

I have used "time machine" simulations to help identify natural leaders in organizations. In this procedure, groups of workers are given challenging assignments that simulate tasks they will face in the future. They are then watched by trained observers, evaluated on the basis of their leadership potential, and coached to take better advantage of their talents and to overcome their deficiencies. When those with talent are encouraged, their self-confidence rises.

Obstacles

Many employees enter work with unrealistic expectations. Some are arrogant about their credentials and past experience. Insecure individuals often find it difficult to receive criticism and coaching. Rising expectations, fostered in part by extensive miseducation, often create impatience among those who need to take time to "learn the ropes." Many career-oriented workers rely too heavily on the organization for "development." Self-reliance is too often missing or in short supply.

Some workers mistake career possibilities and career probabilities, and fail to sense the need for continued growth and adjustment. Many workers fall into nonhuddler patterns and become a negative influence on the informal organization. Nonhuddlers perpetuate themselves through many of the same informal ways as do huddlers. Training provided in-house by organizations and by outside training institutions often fosters nonhuddling and inhibits huddling.

Coaches should work to overcome these problems, beginning with understanding that the obstacles exist.

Other Helping Roles

A number of other "helpers" are available to huddlers, although none play quite so important a role as the coach.

Mentors. In the mentor relationship, the worker is tied very closely to one person, from whom he learns. It is an ongoing, intensive, superior–subordinate relationship. Commitment and loyalty are strong. The subordinate is a protégé. Because of its limited scope of activities, mentoring is not as productive a learning relationship as coaching.

Heroes. Heroes are observed, emulated, and admired by huddlers. However, except in unusual cases, they are too far removed and abstract to provide the developmental models huddlers need. They can motivate and provide general direction, but not day-to-day assistance.

Sponsors. Sponsors can put in a good word for huddlers and sometimes help them obtain desirable work opportunities. This should not be discounted. However, the sponsor is not usually there to provide practical ideas and suggestions once huddlers have the opening they need.

Teachers. Teachers can provide huddlers with ideas, theories, systems, and abstract models. These concepts can be valuable, but they are often presented out of context and do not have clear applicability. Inevitably, such teachings do not fit with the realities of huddling, and the conversion of ideas into practice can be extremely difficult.

Advisers. The adviser takes ideas and translates them for huddlers to fit their unique situations. But advisers too are off-line, not in the same arena as huddlers. They are "once removed" from the actions and responsibilities of huddling.

Guardians. The guardian protects and at times coddles the huddler. While it helps to have someone run interference, huddlers also need help moving through the opening provided or acting properly once the opposition has been quieted.

Stewards. Huddlers should be held accountable for what they do and how they are improving in performance. The steward—a boss, superior, or senior specialist—can take huddlers to task on their work and push them to do better. However, stewards rarely provide the "how to" that is essential for a huddler's growth.

Big brothers. Big brothers offer a shoulder to cry on. When huddlers need to release pent-up feelings, whine, or lick their wounds, the big brother or buddy is the one to find.

The point to remember is that all huddlers need help. They need it when they need it, and in the form that is best suited to their situation. In my experience, the coach combines the best qualities of these various noncoaching helpers and adds the on-the-spot practicality that helps huddlers grow.

Coaching Coaches

Coaches can be developed too—consciously and systematically—though they seldom are. Existing managers with coaching potential can be asked to do more coaching, then trained and prepared for this new responsibility. Some organizations include coaching as part of a manager's formal job description. But this will not help unless the informal organization supports it as well. And managers seldom outgrow their need for coaching. Coach training should be included in supervisory and management training programs in order to build an awareness of the need for coaching and to promote coaching skills.

Coaching skill should be a major criterion in the selection of supervisors. Managements need to develop ways to assess coaching ability and to develop it further. Natural coaches should encourage and support others to assume coaching responsibilities. Indeed, every huddler should be a coach.

External Coaching

The nurturing of coaches generally is ignored by organizations. Since most people do not understand how huddles operate, this is not surprising. Also, many senior executives and political leaders find coaching tremendously challenging and difficult.

External coaches can help senior executives who find it difficult to obtain coaching from within the organization. External help has come from retired executives, management consultants, psychologists, attorneys, doctors, and friendly executives from other organizations. Without firsthand observations or practical diagnostic assistance, external coaches may not always understand the situations faced by the executive. But they do have the advantages of being objective, credible, expert, and removed from the power structure with which the executive is contending.

As outside observers, external coaches often see

ways to make working environments more hospitable for huddlers. A number of intriguing approaches have been tried to help organizations and their officials operate more productively. Three of my experiences will illustrate what I mean:

- ▫ My studies revealed that an agency with two-thirds of one federal department's total annual budget—$8.5 billion—was being run more by the informal than the formal organization. Top management had not been bringing together those who needed to cooperate on critical matters. With some slight variations in formal procedures I was able to change their pattern of huddling. Those who had related official duties were drawn into huddling activities, new relationships, and constructive problem solving. These more productive relationships continue today as a natural result of shared concerns and strengthened personal relationships.

- ▫ I was called into an organization where labor representatives and management were seriously at odds—to the point of engaging in physical conflict. As a neutral party requested to assist by both sides, I met privately with individuals in each of the opposing "camps," then got them together in small groups to discuss some realities of organizational life. Basically, what I explained was my theory of huddling: that formal organizations are frustrating to many people, that power is diffuse, that no one completely controls things, that checks and balances slow things down, and so forth.

  After appealing to each side's sense of fair play and getting a commitment to more tolerant working relationships, I let matters proceed on their own. Since that time, significant improvements in huddling relationships have been evident throughout the organization.

□ The head of a large research and development organization came to me with the complaint that output had dwindled seriously and morale was terrible. The organization had centers throughout the United States involved in research vital to the national interest. The new research programs lacked perspective, were behind the times, and were generally parochial and unimaginative.

In my role as consultant, I assembled representatives from various centers into small teams, asked them to spend two days formulating a research proposal to meet a current need, and had them present the proposal to top management. My staff and I then observed the skills and contributions of each participant and provided private coaching feedback discussions. Participants were also evaluated—by themselves and by outside staff—for leadership and problem-solving skills. This program was followed with numerous groups for about a year.

Through this rather simple procedure, we helped foster a climate conducive to huddling. Participants made new acquaintances and began to initiate task-related discussions. Interdisciplinary work was stressed. Huddling skills were assessed and encouraged. Leadership potential was unearthed and strengthened. Top management began to get better proposals. Participants requested transfers so they could work more closely

with newly found partners. Intercenter cooperation increased. Huddling happened.

Numerous other examples could be given to
demonstrate how huddling can be encouraged, fostered, and improved through coaching. The point is
that very practical means are available to organizations for nurturing huddlers and improving the huddling process.

19
Huddling Hurdles

I N preceding chapters we have examined the origins of huddles, their usefulness to both the informal and formal organization, and ways in which huddlers can more effectively exercise leadership and influence. While the advantages of huddling are clear, problems can and do arise with such a pervasive, unbridled activity. Not all these problems are open to solution. Many huddling "hurdles" are natural consequences of the process—indeed, the very attributes that make huddles work.

Organizational Responsibility

The issue of organizational responsibility goes directly to the origins of huddling itself. Since huddles arise to fill leadership gaps in the organization, these informal activities can sometimes supplant the responsibilities of the formal organization. Many people react to this by simply condemning huddles and divorcing themselves from the informal organization. They are quick to label huddling as "politics." But mere labeling does not resolve the problem. The only solution is to strengthen the formal organization so that the issue is less likely to arise.

Discipline

Many people are disturbed by the lack of discipline inherent in huddling activities. Some have sought to seal off any activities other than the formal operations of the organization. But such attempts have rarely been successful. By their very nature, people will act to get results through extraorganizational means. Indeed, to a large extent the informal organization is "out of control." Except for the affirmative controls and bridling techniques described earlier, very little can be done to ride herd on huddling processes.

Competition

Competition is as much a part of huddling as is cooperation. The very nature of assertive authority and of working enclaves gives rise to a generous amount of rivalry between individuals and work groups. Many people find this competitiveness difficult to accept; they withdraw to avoid the maelstrom of political activities in the huddling milieu. They would be less critical of huddling if they had a better understanding of the constructive role it plays in organizational life.

Private Interests

The question is frequently asked: Whose needs are being met through huddling? Many people feel that private rather than corporate or public interests prevail in the informal organization, that the huddle is a place for self-aggrandizement. This is not so. Because of the competitive nature of the huddle, the private interests of any one individual are usually checked by the private or public interests of others. The natural checks and balances of huddling also limit the likelihood that huddlers will join in "pork barrel" activities.

Sharing the Work

Inclusion in extensive huddling networks may overextend some huddlers. Many huddlers will resist overcommitment. But huddling is not a formal process where the activities of certain individuals can be monitored. Many people appear to be busier than they really are. Activity, productive or not, expands to fill the time that is available. Still, certain people become heavily loaded with formal and informal responsibilities, while others go underutilized. This creates problems not only for the individuals who are underused or overburdened but also for the organization that is trying to be equitable. Huddlers need to monitor their own loads and the burdens they impose on others. They should be alert to signs of unhealthy stress levels: depression, lack of accomplishment, withdrawal.

Visibility

Huddling is hidden from the view of most people. They sense something is happening, but the nature of informal activities is not clear to them. This obscurity occurs, in part, because of the lack of documentation about huddling processes. Huddling deliberations, decisions, and communications usually become visible only through the formal organization. This lack of documentation can ultimately lead some participants astray. Indeed, it has led to the demise of officials in both public and private organizations when huddling has extended into illegal areas.

Checks on Information

Because of the informality of huddling processes, opinions and actions may be based on unnecessarily incomplete data. It can be argued that the data that come through this informal process are more complete and more accurate than the information received by the formal organization. Still, it is risky to assume that the information obtained in huddles is correct.

In some respects, huddling lacks the built-in checks that characterize the information flow in the formal organization. In an informal setting, people sometimes rely too heavily on a few established sources of information and overlook others. This is particularly true when people become smug and are not plugged into a comprehensive huddling network. Huddlers should be aware of the potentially constricted sources of information and should not assume its validity without careful evaluation and broader search for data. Obtaining, testing, and validating information are very important functions of huddles.

Cloning Personnel

Some huddlers perpetuate "their kind" in huddling activities. This is inbreeding, a form of value-oriented nepotism that can weaken both the huddling process and its results. Although comfortable and trusting relationships are important in huddling, the danger of accumulating yes-oriented associates—molding fellow huddlers after one's own personality, and interests—should be recognized.

Accountability

Huddles lack a system for ensuring accountability. This is not to suggest that formal organizations fare much better. But since huddling has no legal authority and is frequently hidden from public scrutiny, there is no check on whether the organization's interests are truly being served. As news reports have indicated, close working relationships sometimes lead to behavior contrary to the public interest.

Meg Greenfield has raised questions about the accountability of informal advisers to the President of the United States—people who have not been elected or officially appointed to office but who are in a position to wield undue influence.* All those who enter into political processes must expect to come under scrutiny and be held accountable for their acts. The same applies to huddlers, who must be ready to stand before the glare of public opinion and organizational inspection.

Due Process

Huddling usually lacks visible "due process"—a systematic means of providing for hearings, adversary proceedings, or public airings to check on decisions and policies. In a sense, the absence of these tech-

* *The Washington Post,* June 15, 1977.

niques is a tribute to the efficiency of the informal organization. The informal organization runs its own course according to the best judgment of those involved, tempered somewhat by the competitiveness of huddling activities.

The competitive give and take of the informal organization generates some control through opposing opinions and through coordination, checking, and clearing with interested individuals. But the absence of *formalized* due process should be a concern among those wielding influence in huddling processes.

Overworked Talent

The most talented people—those who are most capable of making contributions and providing up-to-date information and relevant experience—are going to be in greatest demand within huddling networks. While merit systems of promotion may focus on those with impressive credentials, the real contributors are those who have proved themselves valuable in huddling processes. Since talented performers are in short supply, they usually find themselves with an overload of opportunities. Other people are left to inconsequential activities within the formal organization.

Since inclusion in huddles is an informal process, it is extremely difficult to apportion the time and talents of skilled performers to best serve the needs of the organization. Individuals who are faced with this problem should nurture expertise on the part of others to help move them into the huddling network. They should also resist overcommitment to huddling activities. But it takes more than most people realize to reach the "straw that breaks the camel's back." It is impressive how much an individual with huddling skill and drive can do when highly motivated.

Brain Drain

Huddling has no built-in mechanism for capturing, codifying, storing, or retrieving valued information held by participants. The official organization does provide for this to some extent through files, records, and reports. But normally that information is somewhat disoriented and less valuable than what key individuals carry around in their heads.

Hence, the loss of knowledgeable and experienced huddlers—to retirement, death, other employment, or other activities—can leave the huddling network highly vulnerable. It can also bring about a significant reordering of huddling relationships. To help overcome this problem, huddlers should make an effort to share critical information more widely and to broaden the base of contributors so that huddles do not depend heavily on any single participant.

Ambiguity

A huddle by its very nature lacks official definition. Exact duties are unclear, and individuals are left to carve out their areas of contribution through competition and interaction with others. Because of this ambiguity, people often find it difficult to understand career progression, particularly when rewards are based on technical performance, credentials and education, and past positions. In addition, real working relationships are not always spelled out for new or uninformed participants. Critical activities in the organization are not documented, forcing participants to pick up for themselves information that is valuable in their operations.

"Policies" developed through huddling are usually in the form of understandings. Eventually they may be presented to and incorporated in the official organization, but in the intervening period many workers will not understand what is going on. Also, in most huddles leadership is shifting and unintelligible to many participants and observers. Huddlers can overcome these difficulties to some extent by improving their ability to "read between the lines" and by searching out needed information about influence and centers of power.

Conflicting Demands

Active involvement in huddling may well conflict with demands of the formal organization. The working enclave of one person may compete sharply with the working enclave of others. One person's assertive authority competes with the assertive authority of another. Rewards for contributions are not always commensurate with the actual productivity of those involved. Often, too, individuals who obtain valuable information in huddles are constrained from disclosing it at will.

All these conditions create conflicts for huddlers. Among those who are vulnerable to stress, the outcome is frequently withdrawal, resignation, absenteeism, bickering, lowered morale, physical or emotional breakdown, or unhealthy aggression. These conditions need to be monitored by perceptive and skilled managers.

Transitions

Most organizations have some provisions for orienting new workers—moving them from formal educational institutions into the work organization.

The huddling network has no such set of mechanisms. Orientation occurs through "socialization." Unclear understanding about the informal organization leads many people to condemn huddling as messy, irrational, or political. It also tends to foster cynicism about the organization and its operations.

Discrimination

A serious problem of discrimination can arise in huddles. People can easily and subtly be excluded for extraneous reasons, since no formal controls exist for inclusion in huddling activities. Trust, intimacy, and smooth working relationships are prerequisites for effective huddling. If a huddler has uncomfortable feelings toward minorities, he may inadvertently or consciously exclude them from huddling activities. This can happen even if minority workers are highly skilled and knowledgeable or hold key positions in the formal organization.

Women. In the past huddling in most organizations has worked to the disadvantage of many capable women. One reason has to do with social exclusion, and another with the intimate nature of huddling activities.

Women have not been a part of the old-boy network—the "kitchen cabinet" familiarities, weekend games, after-hours socializing, and chauvinistic joking that create the friendly, comfortable relationships through which networks of power are forged. These patterns will change as more and more women assume key power positions.

In addition, the prevailing mores of the organization may discourage sexual intimacy when it is coupled with task-oriented activities in the work environment. Thus, when sexual feelings may be aroused by an intimate working relationship, as in huddling activities, some degree of sexual exclusion is normal.

This problem can be exacerbated if any of the parties have a reputation for sexual promiscuity; if personal values prohibit male-female working relationships of any kind; if people are concerned about what others may say about such relationships; if people fear sexual involvement at work and want to avoid the possibility altogether; or if a strong sexual attraction exists between co-workers.

Ethnics. Because of common cultural backgrounds, ethnic groups often associate together. Language, humor, religion, geographical orientation, and other bonds help facilitate communications and cooperation.

Just as these circumstances draw people together, so they can produce barriers *between* ethnic groups. People who feel an affinity for others of similar heritage may find it uncomfortable to work with members of different ethnic groups. All huddlers should be aware of this tendency to erect ethnic barriers and should strive to overcome personal biases.

Atypicals. By virtue of the same forces, a variety of other people can be excluded from intimate huddling relationships. Some individuals are dismissed by others as "weirdos"—a judgment that has nothing to do with their competence. Such "threatening" or "repulsive" individuals include homosexuals, lesbians, hippies, religious fanatics, political radicals, and funny dressers.

Any distinctive characteristic can be a basis for exclusion: acne, nervousness, scars, blindness, amputation, bad breath, deafness, body odor, stuttering, cross-eyes, obesity, smoking, ugliness, alcoholism, shortness, or tallness. Again, huddlers must strive to overcome any biases or preferences that are not related to people's ability to work in huddles. At the same time, those with "handicaps"—whatever their nature—should do what they can to minimize any discomfort produced in others.

Other "atypicals" in the organization include those who have unusual responsibilities outside of work. For instance, someone who has a large family or heavy community responsibilities may find it difficult to work extra hours or to engage in the recreational or social activities in which considerable huddling occurs. Even having to meet a car pool can make spontaneous huddling difficult before or after work hours.

Fumblers. People who have made mistakes in judgment in the past may in the future be unfairly excluded from huddles. These are the workers who are out of favor, on the shelf, demoted, disgruntled, turned off, not fully trusted by others. These individuals may have valuable contributions to offer. Huddlers should scrutinize their attitudes to make sure that they are not excluding people solely on the basis of personal grudges or past mistakes. Many of these workers need to be given another chance to prove themselves as contributors to the organization.

I was once contacted by the top management of an organization to assess a number of middle level managers and staff whom management considered to be unproductive troublemakers. I designed an assessment center to serve this purpose, established groundrules to protect those involved, and brought in a "control group" to avoid spotlighting the major purpose of the program.

Following the assessment phase, we counseled in private with each individual and later with employees and their supervisors. We observed that the unproductive troublemakers generally were more talented and capable than those in the control group. It was clear that these people could become significant contributors if they were given another chance by top management and if they developed a more positive view of themselves and the organization. Both of these are possible.

20
Huddle Hints

WHILE providing executive coaching services for the Department of Health, Education, and Welfare, I worked with a man whose unusual leadership skills impressed me tremendously. He was bright, knowledgeable, talented, and obviously respected by his peers. When I visited him in his office, I found my way through a remote area into an almost bare room. Water pipes were exposed, the floor was uncarpeted, there was no window or secretary. The furnishings consisted of a small metal desk, a file cabinet, a telephone, and his chair. We borrowed a second chair and I sat down and listened to his story.

He had risen quickly as a public servant and was appointed to a supergrade rank—equal to that of a general in the military. Then he accepted a politically risky assignment. Although he was successful in his mission, the political climate changed and he was put aside and out of view. That is where I found him. In the official organization he had high rank—a special assistant to an Assistant Secretary. His official duties were totally perfunctory.

But this man was committed to making a contribution in his work. Status and position didn't matter. He volunteered to handle some seemingly innocuous committee assignments, meeting regularly with two national associations in his field. He kept informed about needs, developments, public opinion, and congressional interests. By virtue of what he learned, coupled with his prior experience, he conceived new policies and legislation that changed the character of services offered by the government. Through his continuing huddling opportunities and initiatives—for which he had plenty of time—he was able to quietly work through others to bring changes of national significance.

Keeping a low profile is only part of what it takes to be a skillful huddler. Huddlers must continually sharpen and refine their skills. This chapter presents a number of hints to help you improve your huddling abilities.

Timing

A skillful huddler has the ability to quickly get into and out of huddles. A huddler needs to know when the time is ripe to present an idea, convey a message, seek a decision, or work out an agreement with a colleague. Some people always seem to raise a questionable point at the wrong time and get rebuffed as a result. The effective huddler avoids such errors by being sensitive to the appropriate timing for engaging in interactions with others.

Huddling skills include the ability to ask a provocative question, throw out an illuminating idea, suggest a timely move, or identify a troublesome situation. All these skills help to get a huddle started. Since many huddles are held on the spur of the moment, in between other events, and while other formal demands are pressing, it is imperative to be skillful in initiating a huddle. Timely disengagement from huddles is just as essential as efficient start-up. If you are not able to wrap it up and get out of the huddle, your engagement may be seen as a problem to others in the execution of their responsibilities. If your supervisor has 60 seconds to talk before he's expected in the boss's office, you'll have to slip in to get a decision and get out again within that time. Effective start-up and termination of the huddle are imperative.

Preparation

Huddlers must be prepared. If you have a very short time to spend on a given problem, it is important to have the facts before you, to offer a solution to your problem, and to seek a response. Whatever the subject of the huddle, you and all others who participate should be prepared to focus on the issue at hand, deal with it in a constructive manner, and conclude with some course of action to be taken.

The key to effective huddling is contribution and productivity by those involved. That can come about only through adequate staging, and preparation and a constructive working attitude on the part of all involved.

Adaptability

Since huddling activities are not always predictable, alertness and adaptability are essential. Frequently, while you are busily involved in a project you may get a call to slip over to someone's office. You should be able to quickly shift gears to accommodate reasonable (and sometimes unreasonable) requests. While responding to such a huddle, you may encounter other requests for opinions, facts, or background information. You may be told to stop by for one purpose, then find something else has come up.

The ability to handle problems on short notice, to move from one subject to another, and to act discreetly and constructively at each point in the process makes you a valued member of the huddling team. If you become critical of such stop-and-go activity, you are sure to find yourself excluded from future huddles. Indeed, you should have an attitude of being "in motion," ready to respond and contribute to problems as they emerge.

Authenticity

Be yourself—at your best. Authentic behavior—being what you really are—is a hallmark of the huddling process. This attribute is vital when you are asked to comment on, evaluate, or implement a course of action. In dynamic huddling there is little room for game playing, posturing, or make-believe. Your contributions must be an authentic reflection of your capabilities and personality. And these contributions must be not only *natural* but *effective*—they must enhance the huddling process.

Place

Many people believe that meetings are the most influential events in an organization. This notion needs to be put to rest. Much of the real work of the organization takes place in huddles, and huddles occur best wherever they *can* occur.

One manager told me: "Our division meetings are terrible. Everybody wants to talk, usually about a pet peeve or favorite project. It's like a batch of broken records. I've learned to wait everyone out and then catch the director for a minute after the meeting. Or I see him on the run some other time. We're able to handle our business better that way."

Obviously, if an extremely sensitive matter is to be discussed, discretion dictates a relatively private location. However, "in public" can be very private. Noise can serve as a barrier and provide a degree of insularity.

Often matters are best handled inconspicuously through a brief chance meeting, a walk through the hall, or a discreet phone call, since others will be less likely to catch the full significance of what is being said. A gathering in someone's office may serve as a signal that something is going on and may undercut the effectiveness of the huddle. The important test is whether a particular setting provides the degree of visibility and confidentiality required.

Senator Henry Jackson explained the need for confidentiality as he walked to a private caucus of Senate conferees working on an energy bill: "In order to do the job, we have to have private conversations. Either we are whispering or we go out and have coffee. The real decisions come in private." *

---

* *The Washington Post*, December 11, 1977.

In extended huddles where several individuals gather to deal with many issues, a retreat-type setting may be appropriate. Many businesses and other groups have found it useful to have a few key individuals meet away from the office in a relaxed setting where they can establish rapport, speak frankly, and work informally. Huddles can be held on a plane trip, during a ride to the airport, over a quick lunch, during a coffee break, in the office, in the corridor, or in the rest room. They can occur on the weekend, at a game of golf, after hours in someone's office, or while taking a midday walk.

Many huddles occur naturally and effectively in participants' offices. Much of what goes on does not need to be "undercover." Excessive wrappings of secretiveness or mystery can be detrimental. Again, appropriateness is the key: huddlers must be comfortable with the circumstances they are in. By being sensitive to this need, and by observing others and thinking through your observations, you can exercise good judgment about the setting for huddles.

Accessibility

Huddlers must be accessible to each other. Huddling is severely hampered if co-workers find it difficult to get to each other on the spur of the moment. The specific nature of the huddling network will determine who is accessible to whom. In complex organizations everybody cannot be available at all times to everybody else. Open-door policies have their disadvantages as well as benefits.

The important point for huddlers is this: those who would huddle effectively must be available for personal contact. Some restrictions on the individuals included may be appropriate at times; effective huddlers make themselves accessible to "fit" the circumstances of their working relationships.

Productivity

The informal organization cannot tolerate lack of productivity nearly so well as can the formal organization. Therefore, one of the rules of huddling is to get things done. The huddle is no place for indecision. The absence of real productivity cannot long be disguised. If you are not a contributor, there is no reason for you to be included in future huddles, unless different circumstances would better take advantage of your abilities and interests.

Keep in mind that the nature of people's contributions will vary. Many different attributes, talents, and bits of information are necessary to make the informal organization work. Self-appraisal and careful evaluation of your past performance will help you determine if you are usually a contributor, a neutral bystander, or a detractor in a huddling situation. Contribution to progress and action is a basic ingredient of huddling.

Conflict Among Co-Huddlers

What do you do when you must work with people who do not get along? Not all huddlers are compatible, after all. Normally, however, huddlers are less caught up in hassling and competing than are others in the organization.

Suppose you have two subordinates who are very competitive and mistrustful of each other. Both see their career progress as mutually exclusive. Here are some suggestions:

1. Deal with each person in separate huddles.
2. Involve them in huddles together, but on matters that will make them feel less competitive, with less at stake.
3. Coach them individually and together. Talk through the problem. Elicit more magnanimous attitudes.
4. Give them some groundrules for working with each other and with you: no cutting others down, focus on results, and so on.
5. Bring in another personality, a constructive influence who can help you bring them together.
6. Remember that trust takes time to foster. Don't force it. Build constructive experiences for them.
7. Set a good example. Point out other productive workers who should be emulated.
8. Make needed organizational changes when possible. Remove any rules or structures that may indeed be making their progress mutually exclusive. Don't be too tolerant of obsolete practices in your work environment.

Strategy

Within the huddle, key actors touch base on strategy—the critical action points in their plan. The huddle is the place to anticipate danger faced in the implementation of the plan and to ensure that things occur on schedule.

Huddles convene at critical points in the formation or implementation of strategy. It is essential, therefore, to be able to think strategically and to analyze the strategy proposed, evaluate its applicability, and participate in its implementation.

Huddles focus on decision making, planning, and coordination—not detailed execution and implementation. Huddles may produce an action plan, but generally the minutiae are worked out elsewhere. *Actions within the huddle are by necessity catalytic and strategic.* Otherwise huddles would be overly burdened. Their purpose is to provide direction, build support, and pave the way for subsequent actions.

Opportunity Finding

Huddles depend on personal initiative. Whereas those with authority in the formal organization are assigned specific duties, huddle leadership must seek out opportunities that do not necessarily coincide with their job descriptions.

Too often, people look upon job descriptions as constraints on other actions. Official duties, whatever their nature, are merely the launching pad for influence and leadership. Any worker in the organization is in a position to exercise influence. Even the lowest-level worker has opportunities to bolster morale, foster enthusiasm, offer suggestions, counsel with new employees, and help others handle difficult problems that they are not able to resolve alone.

Contributions in the informal organization constitute the extraordinary opportunities of work. Opportunities will not fall into the lap of those who are trying to "get along" in a job. Too often, opportunities look so much like work that people pass them by— they want to rest a while longer before getting involved. To take advantage of opportunities for leadership, huddlers must be aware of troubles and be ready to act when needed. As General Eisenhower once said, "No great man ever complains of want of opportunity."

Losing Yourself

By now it should be clear that huddles are not mechanical operations. There is no precise, logical set of instructions that will guarantee your success in huddling processes. It is true that you must possess certain skills to function as a huddler. But my experience and observations suggest that something more is involved.

To succeed as a huddler, you must "lose yourself" in the process. Huddling should become second nature to you. Your concern for results should lead you to responsible huddling acts. If you say to yourself, "Today I will become a huddler," you will not be nearly as effective as if you ask, "What can I contribute?" "How can I act most responsibly to get this job done?"

In a very real sense, in order to find yourself as a contributing, sought-after huddler, you must lose yourself in the work.

Time Management

Much has been said about "time management"— how to get more done with time available. Like the efficiency expert of another era, the time management specialist would program managers to excessive efficiency. Overstructuring of management activities can be as ineffective as lack of discipline. Much of what happens in the informal organization is spontaneous, unpredictable. An effective leader makes allowances for huddling activities. If tight scheduling becomes paramount, the danger rises that people with needed information and insights will feel shut off and be forced into other avenues. If your style is too tense and harried, important huddlers will not find it conducive to include you.

Handling Nonhuddlers

As noted in Chapter 4, you need to understand the nonhuddler's attributes and how to handle them. Here are several suggestions:

1. Don't be a nonhuddler yourself. Though you may feel like joining with nonhuddlers at times, resist. You undermine your leadership and influence seriously by resorting to those unproductive tactics.
2. Be a model huddler. Let others see the fruits of being a contributor, a doer.
3. Appeal to higher interests. Arouse interest in the work you are trying to accomplish. Make sure as many people as possible understand your objectives.
4. Try to understand the motives behind nonhuddlers' behavior. Do whatever you can to take care of their underlying needs or fears so they can respond more constructively.
5. Teach how. Some workers want to do better but don't understand what huddling is, how to get started, or what skills to develop. Coaching and patience can help in dealing with many nonhuddlers.
6. Blow the whistle on destructive activities. Don't let things get out of hand.
7. Aid toddlers and shuttlers. Spend time getting them into productive activities. Help to accelerate their growth and contributions.
8. If you can't do something to make non-huddlers more productive, get them out of the way so they cause minimal damage to huddlers who are trying to do the job.

9. Use performance appraisals. Tell nonhuddlers where they stand. Let them know how their behavior is affecting others and the organization as a whole.
10. Recognize the usefulness of some nonhuddlers. Sometimes hobblers can help keep you out of trouble. Hurdlers can help expand your vision and aspirations. Coddlers can protect others when things get excessively rough.
11. Watch for provocations. Caution aggressive, high-profile huddlers who may arouse unnecessary antagonisms and encourage nonhuddling counterreactions.

Tempo

The tempo of organizational activities is affected by a number of factors: deadlines and due dates established by the formal organization, cyclical or recurring events, the perishableness of opportunities, the movements of competitors, and the habits and traditions of the institution.

Organizational leaders can control the tempo of huddling activities by setting timetables, interjecting questions about productivity and results, urging output rather than perfection, and birddogging known laggards. Influencing the tempo of huddling activities is an essential attribute of leadership.

Accurate Information

To be an effective huddler, you must focus on reality, not fantasies. To do this you must have accurate information about the organizations involved in your work—their missions, histories, environments, struc-

tures, major policies and strategies, programs and
products, opportunities, and challenges. In addition,
you should understand the nature of people—their
motivations, behavior in groups, bureaucratic behavior, and individual differences. All this requires
listening, observing, canvassing, and picking up facts
and opinions that will help you contribute effectively.

Your network of associates is also a vital factor in
your work as a huddler. You will do well to understand
the skills, knowledge, prejudices, motives, and goals
of those you are involved with as well as those you
may need to work with in the future.

Admittedly, this is a tall order. For the most part,
these matters are not taught in schools and univer-
sities. So do not become overconfident about your past
education; most likely it has not provided you with
everything you need to be an effective organizational
worker.

Management Systems

Keep in mind that management systems—whether
they be meetings, organization charts, reports, delegations of authority, or work plans—can help people
focus their energies and get things done. Such management systems should be designed not only to aid
the official organization but also to accommodate the
huddling process.

Effective management may start out as careful cal-
culation, but ultimately it comes down to the exercise
of human judgment. Management systems and huddling processes should be so constructed that they
sharpen the judgment of all responsible participants.
All organizations are—as Woodrow Wilson described
government—"not a body of blind forces [but] a body

of men. . . . Not a machine but a living thing." And management specialists should not forget that the purpose of organizations is to get results, not just to make things *orderly*.

Robert Frost once said: "We go to the tennis court to play tennis, not to see if the lines are straight." The same applies to management systems.

Interpersonal Relations

Productive working relationships are vital to effective huddling. Such relationships arise, in part, from the assorted interpersonal skills of those involved. Trust, discretion, loyalty in times of stress, and willingness to work toward the common good are the building blocks of successful huddling.

Effective working relationships are, in part, a function of the *effort* expended to build them. This means that you must go out of your way to become acquainted with others, to understand their personalities, working styles, responsibilities, technical backgrounds, and work experiences. What is required? An ability to accept other people's weaknesses, a commitment to develop common interests, and a willingness to devote time and energy to developing productive working relationships.

Barriers

Watch out for barriers to effective huddling: physical separation, cultural differences, mistrust, excessively high risks imposed on unofficial actions, low commitment to organizational goals, personal prejudices, legal restrictions, and lack of support for organizational activities. Do what you can to ensure that these barriers are not erected or perpetuated unnecessarily.

Inducements

A number of personal actions can be taken to encourage huddling:

1. Focus on results. Don't make organizational structures quite so sacred. Use problem-solving retreats; take strolls (not strides) through the store, office, or plant. Conduct team-building experiences to encourage open interchanges and cooperation among co-workers. Try a matrix organizational setup for certain projects.
2. Conduct less formal staff meetings. Try standup meetings to deal quickly with essential matters, then instruct people to handle other items at other times. Maintain a reasonable open-door policy.
3. Use less formal means of communicating. Rely on face-to-face encounters, handwritten notes, and phone calls rather than on letters and memos. Use first names more and formidable titles less throughout the organization, especially at the top.
4. Be more visible to others. Eat with the troops, smile in public, say hello. Pass the time of day with as many people as possible without wasting valuable time. Expand the group with whom you lunch and play. Pat on the back those who get a job done.
5. Be more accessible. Leave people some "psychological space" for getting to you as a person. Unbutton your blazer or vest; lean back.

Ask people for ideas that you should know about. Go after new huddling relationships you think will help you get results.

Sisterhood

I have a natural disinclination for segregation along irrelevant lines. But as noted in the preceding chapter, women face special troubles in breaking into the man's world of huddling. To the extent possible, I suggest that women apply the principles and techniques reviewed in this book to gain their fullest opportunity to become contributors. In addition, women should make a special effort to develop working relationships with other women and to be on the lookout for female colleagues with huddling potential. By focusing on contributions, not charitable entry, women will find doors opening to them.

Years ago I counseled the woman who became the first superintendent of a major national park. She has since helped to open doors for other "sisters." She has provided them with developmental assignments, talked them up, and coached them, and is looked upon as a positive influence on the careers of others in her occupation. Perhaps you can provide that influence for others or gain the benefit with another sister.

When it comes to your *opportunities* to exercise influence, what other people perceive to be real is what matters. Their image of you will affect their reactions and their willingness to venture with you into huddling activities. Your image is built on your past performance, working style, physical stature, notoriety, contact with other huddlers, and the opinions about you in the minds of leaders. You have a responsibility to build and protect your reputation.

Keeping Current

Because of the unique nature of huddling, it is imperative to keep your knowledge and skills as up to date as possible. Those who have been included in significant huddles cannot "let down." You cannot walk away from huddling relationships and then come back expecting to pick up where you were before. Working relationships change continually. Information becomes outmoded, the structure and personnel of the formal organization shift, issues get reshaped and policies reformulated. Effective participation in huddles depends on your *utility*. You must work continually to close the gaps in your knowledge and to update your contacts and skills.

Occasionally "has beens" will try to reenter huddling relationships by calling up old memories or basking on "old times." Sometimes former contacts and acquaintances will open the door for reentry, but continued participation will always depend on an ability to contribute. *With the door set slightly ajar on the basis of old times, the individual must once again prove himself worthy of the huddling relationship.*

Reentry may require new training, coaching, getting reoriented as quickly as possible, or making new contacts. Everyone must pay attention to the need for continuing education and growth.

Epilogue:
The Huddler's Code

WORKERS have two challenges: one is to be effective in the official organization; the other is to be effective in the huddling process. If workers commit themselves to both these tasks, significant improvements in the quality of working life, services, and products can be achieved. Organizations succeed only when workers are committed to getting results.

What kind of attitude should huddlers have? Are huddlers born or made? Can workers learn to be more influential in huddling with others? Can one individual make a difference in an organization? Without being evangelical, I advocate a positive, optimistic approach. Huddlers can be developed and improved. An individual can make significant differences. In such a posture is hope!

For years I have observed and coached thousands of leaders and aspirants to leadership positions. With confidence, and with their needs in mind, I offer you a "huddler's code" for managing yourself and managing others in the informal organization.

Self-Management

Success in your career depends on self-management and self-control as well as service. Work on several dimensions of yourself that will pay dividends in results and personal satisfaction.

Don't resign yourself to what you are. Everyone can make major improvements in some area of performance. Work environments do not always support individual growth: opposition and conflict are ever present to discourage efforts to improve. However, as an intelligent human being, you have some power to act, not only to be acted upon. And if you believe this about yourself, you can believe it about others. The genius of organizational life is that people working together can accomplish things they could not do on their own.

Give to others. Submerge your own ego when necessary. Relinquish a measure of your own desires in order to work toward the common Good. Remember that your own ideas about work must be translated into huddling strategies, action plans, divisions of responsibilities, and joint efforts for achieving worthy goals.

Be capable. Have something to offer. Work on your skills. Be good at what you do. Keep learning. Weed out bad working habits. Be a doer. Be open to what people are trying to tell you tactfully about how you can improve.

Be available. Be positive. Take initiative. Look around. Be alert to what needs to be done. Don't hold back from getting involved. Think of yourself as a contributor. Cultivate contacts that will enhance your future chances. Work on your reputation. Let your interests and talents be known in discreet ways—without bragging or exaggerating. Stop putting yourself down. Take risks, but make sure they are controlled and intelligent ones.

Avoid pitfalls. Don't look for trouble. Watch your private life. Don't buy the faddish, shifting standards of social behavior. Generally they are shortcuts not to happiness, but to more hassles. Obey the law. Be faithful to your family and worthwhile traditions. Don't buy the idea that your private life is your own business. It will always—always—spill over into your work.

Maintain your integrity. Personal integrity is a critical need in organizations. You will face many situations that threaten your integrity. To guard against compromise, you should hold to the following standards:

— Avoid illegal acts of any kind.
— Don't lie or misrepresent the truth.
— Keep confidences to which you have committed yourself.
— Don't allow personal goals to undermine organizational objectives.
— Resist activity for activity's sake.
— Commit yourself to being productive. Know the difference between hassling, hustling, and huddling.
— Relate your huddling activities to the formal organization whenever possible. Avoid tearing

down the formal dimensions of your work need-
lessly.
— Blow the whistle on moral violations.
— Avoid hurting other people.
— Examine your own prejudices and biases. Pro-
mote equality and fairness whenever you can.
— Contribute a full day's work for whatever pay
you receive.

Don't leave your career in the hands of others.
Some organizations have career development programs. Few work well. Many people who rely on them
get shortchanged. Remember that careers are managed mostly in huddles, not in personnel offices. But
don't ignore the personnel office entirely. Be alert to
what the organization is looking for in employees.
Needs change, so keep awake. Your success will depend on what you have to contribute—your skills,
knowledge, and ideas—as well as on what others
know about you. Pay attention to your continuing development and then market yourself wisely.

Managing Huddles

Can huddling processes be managed? If you want
to try, here are some suggestions:
Teach correct principles. Let people know what
you are trying to accomplish and groundrules you feel
they should observe. Let people know what huddlers
do and how huddling works.
Adapt the official organization to current needs.
Get rid of archaic structures, rules, relationships, job
descriptions, or manuals. Update these matters so they
can better meet the organization's needs and goals.
Make the formal organization work for you and contribute to the results you seek.

Be human. Recognize workers as human beings. Take their ideas and feelings into account. Consider the intrinsic worth of people who are not only producing but trying to build worthwhile lives, maintain self-respect, and find meaning in all they do.

Reward competence and performance. Recognize good efforts but give significant payoffs to those who get results. Don't ignore people who always work with the "pack" while others are out front. Give credit where it is due.

Be a model. Demonstrate appropriate huddling behavior. Develop yourself so you can say, "Do as I'm doing." If you want to cleanse the world, start by sweeping your own doorstep. Be the type of person you want your associates to be. But do so quietly; avoid fanfare and grandstanding.

Foster coaching. Let your subordinates know that they are responsible for nurturing the talent of their people. Reward effective coaches and insightful talent scouts.

Discourage destructive nonhuddlers. Learn the difference between the "actors" and the "performers"—those who go through the motions and those who get results. Help shuttlers bridge the gap between shuttling and huddling.

Be a huddler. To huddle is to choose to get results yourself. Let colleagues know you're out to achieve objectives, not just to assert your authority. Be a doer. Be responsible and quit making excuses. Get into the harness. Pull your load. Work with your people to achieve results. Look for opportunities to do good. Keep your eyes open for ways to help the organization.

Suggested Reading

I HAVE not attempted to trace the bibliographic roots of all my thinking about huddling. If I labored hard enough, I'm sure I could find some connection between virtually every idea in this book and someone else's idea in history. But this book is written for you the reader and this reference list should serve you primarily. So my purpose here is to (1) acknowledge those writings directly connected with ideas I've used and (2) provide you with additional sources in case you want to pursue some topics in greater detail.

Some of you will have read only sparsely the literature on organizations and management. Several good books are available on these subjects and I recommend them to you.

James P. Baughman, ed., *The History of American Management*. Englewood Cliffs, N.J.: Prentice-Hall, 1969.

Douglass Cater, *Power in Washington*. New York: Random House, 1964.

Peter F. Drucker, *The Practice of Management*. New York: Harper and Brothers, 1954.

John Kenneth Galbraith, *The New Industrial State*. Boston: Houghton Mifflin, 1967.

Claude S. George, Jr., *The History of Management Thought*. Englewood Cliffs, N.J.: Prentice-Hall, 1972.

Antony Jay, *Management and Machiavelli: An Inquiry into the Politics of Corporate Life*. New York: Holt, Rinehart and Winston, 1968.

Charles E. Lindblom, *The Intelligence of Democracy: Decision Making Through Mutual Adjustment*. New York: The Free Press, 1965.

Harwood F. Merrill, ed., *Classics in Management*. New York: AMACOM, 1960.

Richard E. Neustadt, *Presidential Power*. New York: John Wiley & Sons, 1962.

Studs Terkel, *Working*. New York: Avon Books, 1975.

David B. Truman, *The Governmental Process*. New York: Alfred A. Knopf, 1965.

I have grouped additional books, along with some of those already cited, by the general topics covered in each chapter.

Chapter 1: Huddling

The best books on points covered in this chapter are Edgar H. Schein, *Organizational Psychology*, 2nd ed. (Englewood Cliffs, N.J.: Prentice-Hall, 1970), particularly Chaps. 4, 5, and 6; and Stewart Thompson, *The Age of the Manager Is Over* (Homewood, Ill.: Richard D. Irwin, 1975).

Chapter 2: Huddling Roots

See Harold G. Leavitt, *Managerial Psychology*, rev. ed. (Chicago: University of Chicago Press, 1964), particularly Chaps. 2, 17, 24, and 25. An old-timer is William J. Whyte, Jr., *The Organization Man* (Garden City, N.Y.: Doubleday, 1956).

Chapter 3: Huddle Watching

Some background for this chapter can be gained from George Homans, *The Human Group* (New York: Harcourt Brace, 1950); and Michael S. Olmsted, *The Small Group* (New York: Random House, 1959).

Chapter 4: Nonhuddlers

Read about hasslers, though not by name, in Qass Aquarius, *The Corporate Prince* (New York: Van Nostrand Reinhold, 1971). Parallels with several nonhuddlers can be found in Michael Maccoby, *Gamesmen: The New Corporate Leaders* (New York: Simon and Schuster, 1976). Another typology of organizational leaders is presented in Eugene E. Jennings, *An Anatomy of Leadership: Princes, Heroes, and Supermen* (New York: Harper and Brothers, 1960).

Other versions of muddling are discussed in Theodore Isaac Rubin, *The Winner's Notebook* (New York: Macmillan, 1967); and Charles E. Lindblom, "The Science of Muddling Through," *Public Administration Review*, Vol. 19 (1959). Mumblers are described in other terms in James H. Boren, *When in*

Doubt, Mumble: A Bureaucrat's Handbook (New York: Van Nostrand Reinhold, 1972).

Chapter 5: Huddling Harbingers

For a far-ranging discussion of these ideas, see Merrill, op. cit., and George, op. cit. Political notions are drawn from Jay, op. cit.; MBO from Drucker, op. cit.; bottoms-up authority from Chester I. Barnard, *The Functions of the Executive* (Cambridge, Mass.: Harvard University Press, 1964); and Theory X and Theory Y from Douglas McGregor, *The Human Side of Enterprise* (New York: McGraw-Hill, 1960).

"Linking pin" theory comes from Rensis Likert, *New Patterns of Management* (New York: McGraw-Hill, 1961). J. Sterling Livingston's ideas are in "Myth of the Well-Educated Manager," *Harvard Business Review*, January–February 1971. Also see Laurence J. Peter and Raymond Hull, *The Peter Principle* (New York: William Morrow, 1969). Organization development (OD) is reviewed in several volumes, including Wendell L. French and Cecil H. Bell, Jr., *Organization Development* (Englewood Cliffs, N.J.: Prentice-Hall, 1973).

Chapter 6: Huddle Blindness

Personnel selection and self-appraisal are discussed in numerous personnel management books. See, for example, Edwin A. Fleishman, *Studies in Personnel and Industrial Psychology*, rev. ed. (Homewood, Ill.: Dorsey Press, 1967). For a brief background on the use of simulation techniques to assess leadership dimensions, see Cabot L. Jaffee, *Effective Management Selection* (Reading, Mass.: Addison-Wesley, 1971). Ideas about getting leaders into situations where they can succeed are presented in Fred E. Fiedler, *A Theory of Leadership Effectiveness* (New York: McGraw-Hill, 1967).

Chapter 7: Assertive Authority

For additional pointers on informal authority, see Robert Townsend, *Up the Organization* (Greenwich, Conn.: Fawcett Publications, 1970); Laurence J. Peter, *The Peter Prescription* (New York: William Morrow, 1972); and Herbert Fensterheim and Jean Baer, *Don't Say Yes When You Want to Say No* (New York: Dell Publishing, 1975).

Chapter 8: Working Enclaves

See Livingston, op. cit.; Max S. Wortman, Jr., and JoAnn Sperling, *Defining the Manager's Job* (New York: AMACOM, 1975); Marvin Bower, *The Will to Manage* (New York: McGraw-Hill, 1966); and Leavitt, op. cit.

Chapter 9: Affirmative Control

Motivation theory is helpful here. See Frederick Herzberg, *Work and the Nature of Man* (New York: New American Library, 1973); Leavitt, op. cit.; and Abraham H. Maslow, *Toward a Psychology of Being* (Princeton, N.J.: D. Van Nostrand, 1962).

Chapter 10: Huddle Territory

Discussions on a number of these points can be found in Charles B. Handy, *Understanding Organizations* (Baltimore: Penguin Books, 1976); Leavitt, op. cit.; and Schein, op. cit.

Chapter 11: Huddle Relationships

Sources for follow-up reading include Leonard R. Sayles, *Managerial Behavior* (New York: McGraw-

Hill, 1964); and Max Gunther, *The Luck Factor* (New York: Macmillan, 1977).

Chapter 12: Huddle Decision Making

Decision premises are introduced in Herbert A. Simon, *Administrative Behavior: A Study of Decision-Making Processes in Administrative Organizations* (New York: Macmillan, 1961). Involvement with others in decisions is covered in Robert R. Blake and Jane S. Mouton, *Group Dynamics: Key to Decision Making* (Houston, Tex.: Gulf Publishing, 1961); Leavitt, op. cit.; and Peter F. Drucker, *The Effective Executive* (New York: Harper & Row, 1967).

Chapter 13: Communicating in Huddles

Good background readings include Leavitt, op. cit.; Edward T. Hall, *The Silent Language* (Garden City, N.Y.: Doubleday, 1959); and an excellent little book called *The Communication of Ideas*, published and distributed free by the Royal Bank of Canada, Montreal 101, Quebec.

Chapter 14: Huddling Roles

A basic reference book on role theory is Bruce J. Biddle and Edwin J. Thomas, eds., *Role Theory: Concepts and Research* (New York: John Wiley & Sons, 1966). Some aspects of roles in group activities are outlined in Kenneth D. Benne and Paul Sheats, "Functional Roles of Group Members," *The Journal of Social Issues*, Spring 1948.

Chapter 15: Bridling Huddles

For additional ideas about huddle bridling, see Townsend, op. cit.; Mortimer R. Feinberg, *Effective Psychology for Managers* (Englewood Cliffs, N.J.:

Prentice-Hall, 1964); and Lester R. Bittel, *The Nine Master Keys of Management* (New York: McGraw-Hill, 1972).

Chapter 16: Huddling Agenda

My approach on this matter was stimulated by Marion J. Levy, Jr., "The Functional Requisites of Any Society," in *The Structure of Society* (Princeton, N.J.: Princeton University Press, 1952). Some ideas about how these matters are dealt with at General Motors are found in Alfred P. Sloan, Jr., *My Years with General Motors* (Garden City, N.Y.: Doubleday, 1963). See also Robert L. Katz, *Management of the Total Enterprise* (Englewood Cliffs, N.J.: Prentice-Hall, 1970); and Roland Mann, ed., *The Arts of Top Management* (New York: McGraw-Hill, 1971).

Chapter 17: Huddle Leadership

Aspects of huddle leadership are discussed in Ralph M. Stogdill, *Handbook of Leadership* (New York: The Free Press, 1974); David W. Ewing, *The Managerial Mind* (New York: The Free Press, 1964); Henry Mintzberg, *The Nature of Managerial Work* (New York: Harper & Row, 1975); Barnard, op. cit.; and McGregor, op. cit. You may also enjoy reading James David Barber, *The Presidential Character* (Englewood Cliffs, N.J.: Prentice-Hall, 1972); and Warren G. Bennis, *The Unconscious Conspiracy* (New York: AMACOM, 1976).

Chapter 18: Coaching Huddlers

Useful readings include William G. Dyer, *Modern Theory and Method in Group Training* (New York: Van Nostrand Reinhold, 1972); Robert L. Craig, ed., *Training and Development Handbook*, 2nd ed. (New

York: McGraw-Hill, 1976); Marvin D. Dunnette, *Personnel Selection and Placement* (Belmont, Cal.: Wadsworth Publishing, 1966); and Leonard Nadler, *Developing Human Resources* (Houston, Tex.: Gulf Publishing, 1970).

Literature on coaching—in the context used in this book—is hard to find. You may benefit from some discussions in Marion S. Kellogg, *What to Do About Performance Appraisal,* rev. ed. (New York: AMACOM, 1975); and Ferdinand F. Fournies, *Coaching for Improved Work Performance* (New York: Van Nostrand Reinhold, 1978).

Chapter 19: Huddling Hurdles

Two books on stress are pertinent: Don Gowler and Karen Legge, eds., *Managerial Stress* (New York: John Wiley & Sons, 1975); and Robert L. Kahn, et al., *Organization Stress: Studies in Role Conflict and Ambiguity* (New York: John Wiley & Sons, 1964). Two volumes expanding on my short discussion of women and huddling are Rosalind Loring and Theodora Wells, *Breakthrough: Women into Management* (New York: Van Nostrand Reinhold, 1972); and Letty Cottin Pogrebin, *Getting Yours: How to Make the System Work for the Working Woman* (New York: Avon Books, 1975).

The issue of public interest versus private interest may become clearer by reading Thomas Landon Thorson, *The Logic of Democracy* (New York: Holt, Rinehart and Winston, 1962); George Albert Smith, Jr., and John Bowers Matthews, Jr., *Business, Society, and the Individual,* rev. ed. (Homewood, Ill.: Richard D. Irwin, 1967); and "Today's Executive: Private Steward and Public Servant," *Harvard Business Review,* March–April, 1978.

Chapter 20: Huddling Hints

References here could cover the waterfront. A few include Feinberg, op. cit.; Townsend, op. cit.; James J. Cribbin, *Effective Managerial Leadership* (New York: AMACOM, 1972); R. Alec Mackenzie, *The Time Trap* (New York: AMACOM, 1972); Drucker, *The Effective Executive*, op. cit.; Kellogg, op. cit.; George M. Prince, *The Practice of Creativity* (New York: Collier Books, 1970); and Thomas L. Quick, *Person to Person Managing* (New York: St. Martin's Press, 1977).

Index